Own, Don't Owe Your Future!

Also by Bolaji Olagunju

Hiring Right: *A Matter of Life and Death for Businesses, Business Owners and Executives* (www.hiringrightbook.com)

You Must Become a Trainer: *How to leverage your expertise, experience, and education in any field to do what you love, impact lives, create wealth and own your future.*

Own, Don't Owe Your Future!

26 Vital Lessons for Beating the Odds & Succeeding in Life, Career and Business

BOLAJI OLAGUNJU

Founder, Workforce Group and OwnersInstitute.com

Published by Lift Publishing

Copyright 2021 ©Lift Publishing

Cover and interior design: Shayo Ajiborisha

Hardcover ISBN: 978-1-7339779-1-3

Paperback ISBN: 978-1-7339779-2-0

Digital ISBN: 978-1-7339779-3-7

First edition: August 2021

DEDICATION

This book is dedicated to all the extraordinary individuals who go beyond the call of duty to take full ownership for the lives and responsibilities placed in their care:

To parents who give their all and then some to make this world a better place by raising hardworking and selfless men and women who take ownership, the world has hope because of you. Thank you for your service.

To educators who deliver more value than is expected of them, to teach is to mold a life forever, thank you for your service.

To students who have found out what the best is and strive to do that best, you are our next generation of leaders and professionals, the future of this world rests on you. Thank you for your diligence.

To entrepreneurs who conceive great ideas, and with blood and sweat birth those ideas into great businesses, you are the trees that shelter billions of birds. Thank you.

To employees who take ownership, give their all and render the BEST possible service even when no one is watching, you are the real heroes of the workplace. We doff our hats. Thank you.

To business leaders who take ownership, who love and grow the business on behalf of the owner(s), you are the examples of what leaders should be. We honor you.

To religious leaders who selflessly nurture and nourish the souls of men, you are the balm of the earth. Thank you for your service.

To elected public servants and political leaders who remain faithful in an unfaithful world, you are the force that keeps the wheels of this world running. Thank you for your faithfulness.

To our medical personnel, front line workers, law enforcement officers and military men and women who put their lives at risk every day to keep us safe and to keep law and order in the society, you make the ultimate sacrifice. You will always have our deepest respects. Thank you so much.

To the unsung heroes of our society, the ones who selflessly tend our communities, care for the sick, the aged, the disadvantaged, the orphans and the homeless, you are the finest of us! Our souls bless you. Thank you for all that you do.

To all of you we say:

"Mortals rejoice that so great an ornament to the human race exists."

CONTENTS

INTRODUCTION

The Phenomenon

Not so long ago, I was involved in interviewing a senior Sales & Business Development professional for one of our top business clients. Going by all the basic metrics—experience, skills, carriage, and assessment results, this gentleman was already looking like an ideal fit for the role. And as we progressed with the interview, his confidence, and the responses he gave to the questions we posed him, corroborated our first impressions. All seemed to be going well until I asked him the bubble bursting question.

"Why are you planning to leave your current job?" I asked.

Without hesitation, he replied that he was looking to leave because the company he worked for still owed him his sales commission. I was somewhat puzzled by that response, wondering how anyone ever hoped to motivate a Sales & Business Development employee by withholding their commission. I decided to probe further.

"You mean that the company is violating its agreement to pay you your earned commission?"

"Yes," he replied.

"Are you saying that you have met your sales targets, but they are withholding your commission?" I responded as my brows furrowed.

"Not exactly," he retorted.

"What do you mean, please?" beckoning him to elaborate.

"It is not possible to fully meet those targets."

At this point, the confusion I felt inside must have begun to show on my face and I am sure my fellow interviewers were in the same boat as me.

To get further clarity, I asked, *"If I understood you correctly, are you saying that you are not meeting the set targets and that is the reason for your employers not paying you the agreed commission?"*

"Well... yes," he hesitantly nodded in agreement.

"Please help me understand," I continued. *"How exactly is the refusal to pay you unearned commission the fault of the company?"* I asked in sheer disbelief.

A Destructive Mentality

As we speak, there is an under-the-radar, fast spreading and debilitating disease ravaging the world today. It is far more insidious than all known diseases combined for two main reasons. First, it is not only injurious to the body, but it is also severely damaging to the human psyche—mind, soul, and spirit—the very source of productivity, innovation, and creativity which has enabled mankind fight off physically devastating diseases and pandemics for centuries. Symptoms of this malady are that it prevents people from taking the initiative, making the most of their potentials, and applying themselves and their intelligence to shape and direct the course of their lives.

The second reason why this disease is so cruel is that it often goes undetected for a long time until it has completely crippled its hosts, be they individuals, families, organizations, or nations. It is like an invisible parasitic ghost, difficult to see in solid form, but progressively eating its way into every facet of human endeavor—education, relationships, work, family, business, governance, and religion. Millions of individuals are performing far below their potentials because of this enemy. Many relationships are on the verge of breakdown, and thousands of businesses are struggling to survive and make the most of the huge opportunities available to them, all because of this disease.

The nature of this disease is so sinister that it claims victims both young and old, rich and poor, white and black. It spreads like wild bush fires, causing not only a loss of livelihood, but also a loss of lives on an alarming scale. It is difficult to imagine a more destructive threat.

And what is this devastating disease, you curiously ask? It is the ***Entitlement Mentality***.

Back to the story of my unbelievable encounter with such a senior executive.

Upon seeing the astonished look on my face, he continued emphatically, *"Sir, everyone knows how hard things are in the country. I expect them to still pay my sales commission because they know how hard I work."*

When Lee Siegel, professor emeritus of religion, said, *"I react very badly when mediocrity throws a tantrum of entitlement"*, I completely understood what he meant.

It took a lot to restrain myself from saying to him exactly what I felt and thought about his attitude. Knowing that there was no point in continuing the interview, I stood up immediately signifying the end of the interview and thanked him for coming.

Right there in front of me was a perfect example of the **Entitlement Mentality** on display. Sadly, this sort of encounter with people who believe that the world owes them is not uncommon.

Psychologists say that the entitlement mentality has its roots in narcissism. Some have speculated that it is traceable to the individual's upbringing. Amidst the speculations, they have however defined it as "a sense of deservingness or being owed a favor when little or nothing has been done to deserve the special treatment. It is the 'you owe me' attitude". People with this mindset believe that the world owes them something in exchange for nothing. They view privileges as their rights.

Entitlement Mentality in the Workplace

Peter F. Drucker once said, "*Whenever you see a successful business, someone once made a courageous decision.*" And I will add to that, 'a lot of sacrifice'.

After 20 years of building a business, and relating with other businesspeople, I know for a fact that it is almost impossible to build a successful business without the ingredients of loads of courage and tons of sacrifice. This is therefore what makes the entitlement mentality a bitter pill to swallow for the employer or business owner.

When this toxic mentality shows up in the workplace, it is called 'employee entitlement', and it often manifests as an audacious expectation to do less quality work in less time for more pay and more perks. Unfortunately, a lot of people today want that, desiring promotion, flexibility, balance, meaning, and praise for their work without having earned it.

When you encounter the abysmal performer who brazenly requests for a severance package after being fired, you have met an entitled person. When dealing with the salesperson who demands for a bonus even after failing to meet the agreed sales target, you are dealing with the entitlement mentality. When you find yourself trying to reason with the employee who demands that the company still provides the 'customary' end of year gift package even when they are fully aware that the company has suffered a massive financial loss that year, your struggle is against the entitlement mentality. When your key executives clamor for the company to take a loan to pay salaries when they know fully well that the business is on the verge of bankruptcy, you are dealing with a chronic caseload of the entitlement mentality.

In addition to these examples, the entitlement mentality is often characterized by a lack of appreciation for the sacrifices of others, a lack of personal responsibility, an inability to accept that actions carry consequences and ultimately, increased dependency on others' interventions to solve personal and work problems.

Taking a Stand Against the Entitlement Mentality

I believe one of my life's missions is to eradicate the entitlement mentality and I have vehemently fought against it all my working life. Wherever I encountered it, be it in my organization or in those of my clients, I have worked hard to expunge it because it is destructive to say the least, and worse than a cancer to the growth of that organization. Entitlement destroys motivation, initiative, productivity, and progress.

Every single achievement and progress that mankind has recorded was made on the altar of *effort* and *sacrifice,* which the entitlement mentality strongly resists. It therefore follows that there can be no progress or achievement without a head-on collision with this mentality. For as long as we tolerate this toxic mentality, whether in ourselves or in those that we work with, we can never make progress—at least not at the level that is potentially possible.

This is a book about making progress. I believe very strongly that at every given point in life, we are either climbing up or sliding down the ladder of progress. And whether we are advancing or receding depends on the zone we choose to operate from.

Over the last two decades of operating as a business owner, recruiter, business consultant, coach, mentor, and trainer, I have systematically studied people that were exceptionally successful and carefully observed those who were not so successful. (Success for me goes beyond finances; it extends to the entire well-being of a person including their health and close relationships.) I have also deliberately examined those who always seemed to be struggling with making any kind of headway in their lives. From all of these, I have concluded that the quality of people's lives is directly tied to their decision to operate from either one of four zones: the Entitled Zone, the Comfort Zone, the Performance Zone, and the Ownership Zone. I call them the **Four Zones of Progress**, which will be discussed in Chapter 1 to lay the foundation for this book.

Why I Wrote this Book

When I set out to write ***Own, Don't Owe Your Future***, I had three goals in mind:

Goal One: Expose the destructive nature of the Entitlement Mentality.

Goal Two: Divulge the powerful secrets of the Ownership Mentality.

Goal Three: Provide you with a practical demonstration of how you can take ownership of your future and beat the odds in life, career, and business.

I hope that I succeed in doing these three things. I also hope that you are deeply encouraged by those lessons that conveyed my struggles and disappointments. I hope that they help you realize that tough times, rough patches, and difficulties come to everyone with no exception. More importantly, I hope that you have a renewed sense of focus to pursue your dreams.

By practically demonstrating how I took ownership of my life, I want to show you how you can take ownership of your life, through the lessons in this book which are drawn from my twenty-year entrepreneurial journey. The stories I share are true with names changed or withheld to protect individual and organizational privacy. My hope is that you will read these lessons, fully grasp the meaning of the concept of *Ownership Thinking and Acting* (I go into this further later in this book) and go forward to truly 'own' your life.

Taking ownership of my life in the ways that I will demonstrate in the following chapters completely revolutionized the quality of both my personal and professional life. It is my hope that these lessons will deeply enrich your life too.

CHAPTER 1

TO MAKE PROGRESS, YOU MUST TAKE OWNERSHIP OF YOUR LIFE

"There are two primary choices in life: to accept conditions as they exist or accept the responsibility for changing them."

- Denis Waitley

The Four Zones of Progress

As I said in the introduction, the quality of a person's life is directly tied to their decision to operate from either one of the following four zones.

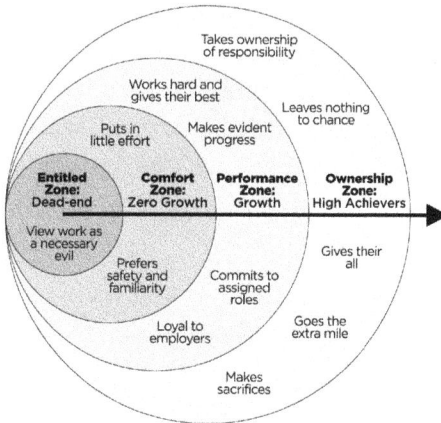

Figure 1: The The 4 Zones of Progress

Zone 1 — The Entitled Zone

Individuals operating from this zone fashion their entire lives following the attributes of the entitlement mentality. To people in this zone, work, wherever it may be required, is a necessary evil. Work is not something that they do with pride, but something that they disdain, try to shortcut, or avoid all together. Entitled people never sharpen their skills, never focus their efforts, and never make the required effort to amount to anything worthwhile. They are the ones in organizations who are not really contributing to its growth, but are still expecting to get their regular pay, and even promotion. Sadly, this is the worst zone to operate from because ultimately no one can ever make any kind of progress from here as it brings nothing but pain and sorrow.

The Entitled Zone is the lowest of all the progress zones. The entitled person cannot go far in life, career, or business because even when they unintentionally gain some advantage, their mentality will get in their way, and they will always end up betraying themselves to their default mode of operation.

Zone 2 — The Comfort Zone

The Oxford Languages dictionary defines the comfort zone in two ways as "a situation where one feels safe or at ease"; and as "a settled method of working that requires little effort and yields only barely acceptable results."

If we combine both definitions, it will read as follows: The comfort zone is a settled method of working that requires little effort, makes one feel safe or at ease, but yields only barely acceptable results. From this definition, it is obvious that the 'comfort zone' is only a little higher than the 'entitled zone'. Inhabitants of this zone are slightly better than those in the entitled zone because they have at least agreed to make some effort. The challenge is that they do not make the amount of effort that is required and necessary to make substantial progress. In choosing to only do those tasks and routines that are familiar and 'safe', permanent residents of the comfort zone spend all their lives using a limited set of skills and behaviors to deliver the same level of performance year in, year out.

The typical mantra of people in this zone is, "I don't like to take risks because I don't like to fail." They imagine the worst-case scenario and opt to stay safe and well tucked in their comfort areas. Unfortunately, staying in a place where there are no challenges or risks always amounts to a life of mediocrity and stunted growth.

By refusing to exert themselves in doing new things, people in the comfort zone deprive themselves of opportunities to grow, and to develop coping mechanisms and the resilience that is needed to survive and thrive.

Zone 3 — The Performance Zone

For people in this zone, the goal is just to perform the job. It is about following orders and getting things done. Performers give their best, work hard at what they are assigned and do enough to produce the expected results.

Performers are typically loyal to and invested in whatever vision that they commit themselves to. They are in for the long haul. When they are assigned tasks, they get the job done quickly, cheerfully, and completely. In the workplace, if it were not for this category of hard-working individuals who help to take care of the business, many of today's great businesses, both big and small, would not be successful at all.

In their personal lives, performers display the same depth of commitment to their growth; they put in sufficient effort to push past their comfort zones to achieve their desired goals. Operating in the Performance Zone is great and rewarding with lots of progress evident. However, it is still short of the ultimate level of progress zone.

Zone 4 — The Ownership Zone

Individuals operating from this zone have an owner's mentality, which means that they take total ownership and complete responsibility for every, single thing that is placed within their charge, including their lives, their jobs, and their future.

'Owners' leave nothing to chance. They are never content to give just their 'best' to what has been assigned to them; they give their ALL! For them, it is all or nothing. Owners do not view tasks as a job, they view it as an extension of their identity; therefore, they approach it with the mindset of 'everything is at stake, and failure is not an option'.

When they are employees, they love and take the business they work for like it is their very own. As a result, they hold nothing back neither physical nor mental energy. They cheerfully do things that others will not do, not because of their position, or because they have financial equity in the organization, but because of their owner's mindset. For them, taking the initiative, going the extra mile, and making sacrifices to see their goals achieved is the only viable way of life that they know. They are not merely committed to the vision of the organization; they adopt and imbibe the vision as theirs.

In their personal lives, 'owners' bring the same energy and approach to the coordination of their affairs. They own their responses to the responsibilities and challenges of life and go above and beyond to see their biggest dreams come true.

In my experience, operating from the 'Ownership Zone' is the only way to make great things happen in life, because taking complete ownership of your outcomes by holding yourself accountable is the single most powerful thing you can do to drive your success.

I wrote this book to help you get into and stay in the 'Ownership Zone' because this is where the biggest opportunities for progress lies.

The Ownership Phenomenon

One of the greatest misconceptions I have come across is the belief that owning something makes you the true owner of that thing. Nothing could be further from the truth. 'Owning' and 'taking ownership' of a thing, referred to as legal ownership and psychological ownership respectively, are two completely different realities.

We all know or have heard of irresponsible parents, politicians, and presidents who fail to take care of the things that they supposedly own. We also know of their relatively few counterparts who take absolute and total ownership of the things in their care and create incredible and lasting impact. It is therefore vital to differentiate between 'owning something' and 'taking ownership of something'.

I am one of the living proofs that when you give your ALL to whatever you do, whether it is in the running of a small business, the dutiful performance of a task assigned to you at your office, or the diligent care of whatever has been put in your charge, the Universe and its resources rise to support you and cause you to make progress. This is no exaggeration. The longer I live, the more I realize that there is a programming in the fabric of the Universe, a force that responds to those who operate from the Ownership Zone—those who take diligent care of their responsibilities and practice a principle that I now call Ownership Thinking and Acting.

I am thoroughly convinced that this force that rises to the aid of anyone who truly and wholeheartedly commits himself to excellence is as real as the force of gravity and all the other immutable forces of nature that hold the Universe together. Neither you nor I can break these laws, the best we can do is to cooperate with them for our safety and our progress.

My insight into the phenomenon of Ownership Thinking and Acting evolved from my personal experience and those of highly successful people whom I have had the privilege of interacting with and learning a whole lot from. Based on these experiences, I have developed the following hypotheses about the power of Ownership Thinking and Acting. I call them Owners' Secrets.

Secret 1
Heaven helps those who take absolute ownership

I am convinced that if God has special favorites, they are the people who take extreme ownership of whatever positive thing that they are doing. This stance comes from my long-term observation that the more I took ownership of a situation, the more divine support I received.

In two decades of running my business, I have made every mistake possible and then some, including mistakes of devastating proportions. So, without meaning to sound religious, I am utterly persuaded that the only reason why I still stand, and my business still runs today is because I am deeply favored by God. And this in turn is because I take complete ownership of most things that I do. It must be the reason, there is simply no other rational explanation.

Secret 2
Humans favor those who take absolute ownership

There is absolutely nothing that can get people rooting for you like when you take total ownership of the things you do. I know for a fact from personal experience that no matter the human endeavor, be it in relationship, sports, business, or social work, ownership signified by dedicated efforts, commitment, and consistency, will always win people's hearts, and repeat business. The potency of this phenomenon becomes even more obvious when you take extreme ownership of things that are not yours. A good example is when an employee operates in their job as if they owned the company, or a consultant works on her client's projects as if the business belonged to her. In any clime, culture or situation, preference will always be given to those who take ownership over those who do not.

Secret 3
Life generally favors those who take absolute ownership

I have witnessed this play out so often in my life and the lives of others enough for me to come to a resounding conclusion that the key to sustainable success in life, career and business is Ownership Thinking and Acting. Believe me when I tell you that seen and unseen forces come to the aid of those who give their best and beyond.

Your Life Ownership Test

Take the survey below to find out how well you are currently taking ownership of your life including your career and business.

I have identified 21 behavioral traits that separate true owners from the rest and have labelled these traits the Ownership Index.

The Ownership Index of a person is the greatest determinant of their performance and ultimately, the results they achieve in any endeavor. I designed the Ownership Index Scorecard as a guide to help you assess the extent to which you are currently adopting key ownership behaviors and taking full and total control of your life, career, or business.

For each of the 21 behavioral traits, I have given two extreme behavioral descriptions. One extreme describes the undesirable ownership behavior while the other describes the desirable ownership behavior. I have also provided a scale from 1 - 10 for rating the extent to which the two extremes closely describe your behavior on each trait.

For instance, if the description on the left better matches your behavior for a particular trait, your rating will range from 1 - 4 depending on how close the match is. If the behavioral description on the right is a better fit to your behavior, your rating should be between 6 and 10. A rating of 5 represents a mid-point.

Scoring Instructions

Add up the numeric value of your ratings for each of the behavioral traits. The maximum possible score is 210. Use the grading below to assess your Ownership Index.

As you take this survey, I am going to ask only two things of you:

1. Be open-minded,

2. Answer all questions with complete honesty.

	Low									High	
Trait 1 – LEVEL OF CARE											
Cannot be bothered about most things. Takes critical issues for granted. Uses phrases like "I can't kill myself." "I am doing my best; it is not my business."	1	2	3	4	5	6	7	8	9	10	Cares more than others think is wise. Believes in first finding out and then doing what the best is. Takes full and total ownership of everything they are involved with.
Trait 2 - RESULTS ORIENTATION											
Equates activities and words to results. Has a strong desire and expects to be rewarded for activities, not results. Wants to be praised, even celebrated for activities. Delivers excuses rather than results. Motto is follow-up.	1	2	3	4	5	6	7	8	9	10	Understands that words and activities are what they are; only result is reality. Very result focused. Wants only to be rewarded and celebrated for meaningful results produced. Delivers results, not excuses. Motto is follow-through.
Trait 3 – BIAS FOR ACTION											
After all is said and done, more is said than done. Talks more than acts. Believes having a lot of ideas is the secret to success. Hardly acts on what is known and always looking for silver bullets. Believes in doing as little as possible. Struggles with decision making – suffers paralysis by analysis.	1	2	3	4	5	6	7	8	9	10	Doesn't believe in talk but no action. Acts consistently towards goals. Understands the secret to success as implementation, not ideas. Knows that one idea well executed is better than many unexecuted ideas. Acts on what is known; doesn't look for silver bullets. Does what it takes to succeed. Very decisive, isn't paralysed by over analysis.
Trait 4 – SELF DRIVE											
Looks for external stimuli/ extrinsic motivation to get going. Must be reminded or pushed to accomplish tasks. Demands less from self than others demand of them.	1	2	3	4	5	6	7	8	9	10	Motivation is internal/ intrinsic, no need for external stimuli. Never needs to be reminded to get things done. Demands much more from self than others can ever demand of them.

	Low	High
	Trait 5 – PERSONAL LEARNING AND DEVELOPMENT	
Cannot be bothered to invest time and money in learning. Ignores continuous learning and development. Only believes in studying for exams/qualifications. Prefers guesswork and speculations. Sees learning as a difficult task, prefers TV or mindless social media activities.	1 2 3 4 5 6 7 8 9 10	Student for life, committed to lifelong, continuous learning and improvement. Willing to go to school on biggest opportunities and challenges facing their progress. Understands the true cost of mindless TV and social media. Knows the importance of superior ability to the attainment of success.
	Trait 6 – RELENTLESSNESS	
Gives up at the first sign of challenges or obstacles. Always looking for easy routes. Doesn't want to operate out of comfort zone. Prefers convenience and fun to the pursuit of worthy goals. Wants everything to be effortless. Will pick easy over challenging.	1 2 3 4 5 6 7 8 9 10	Uses obstacles as steps towards attaining worthy goals. Thrives in discomfort; embraces 'no pain, no gain' philosophy. Has exceptional work ethics and knows that hard work trumps talent. Keeps going in the face of daunting challenges till goal attainment. Takes on challenges knowing there's no growth without pressure.
	Trait 7 – RESOURCEFULNESS	
Always looking for crutches. Believes progress is not possible without more and more resources. Spends more time, effort, energy on raising funds than creating value. Doesn't know how to use what is available to get what is required. Never draws from inner resources, always looking first on the outside for handouts.	1 2 3 4 5 6 7 8 9 10	Knows that resourceful and not more resources is the key to sustainable growth and results. Creates value first before expecting more resources or support. Can make the most of available resources to achieve more with less. Looks inward first for hidden assets that can be leveraged to create and capture value.

Low		High
Trait 8 – STANDARDS OF EXECUTION		
Has a mindset of anything goes. Not committed to high standards of excellence and performance. Inconsistent in quality of output. Adopts personal or local definition of excellence.	1 2 3 4 5 6 7 8 9 10	Dedicated to the highest standards of excellence & performance. Doesn't ever compromise on quality standards. Never cuts corners. Adopts universal definition of excellence. Understands that excellence has only one global definition.
Trait 9 – LEAVING THINGS TO CHANCE		
Expects things to go as planned, hardly gives consideration or any thought to plan B or contingency plans. Overly optimistic.	1 2 3 4 5 6 7 8 9 10	Knows that professionals do not leave things to chance, always has plan B and C in case plan A doesn't work out. Productively paranoid.
Trait 10 – ATTITUDE TOWARDS FAILURE		
Very risk-averse, terrified of failing. Worried about what people will say or think. Prefers to play it safe. Uncomfortable with uncertainty and wants predictability.	1 2 3 4 5 6 7 8 9 10	Willing to take calculated risks. Doesn't care what people think. Understands failure as part of the process of achieving success. Very comfortable with uncertainty and knows predictability is a myth; nobody can predict the future.
Trait 11 – ADAPTABLE		
Abhors change. Has strong immunity to change. Prefers status quo. Doesn't observe changes in the environment and never adapts. Likes to play victim and blames external happenings on fortune and results.	1 2 3 4 5 6 7 8 9 10	Understands that the only constant in life is change. Embraces change, adapts before it becomes necessary. Constantly monitors the environment and adapts as required. Takes personal responsibility for fortune and results.

Low		High
	Trait 12 – KEEPING COMMITMENTS & AGREEMENT	
Struggles to keep commitments due to overcommitting, legitimate reasons or poor planning. Promises made are not promises kept. Seldom meets up with set deadlines.	1 2 3 4 5 6 7 8 9 10	Knows that promises made must be promises kept. Their word is a bond. Keeps promises, no excuses. Thinks whatever it takes. Where impossible to keep promises, renegotiates before deadline.
	Trait 13 – FOCUS ON SERVING OTHERS	
Self-focused. Always looking out for own interest first and primarily. Doesn't do anything except there is some reward involved. Very transactional in orientation. "What's in it for me" orientation.	1 2 3 4 5 6 7 8 9 10	Primary focus is on serving others. Understands that the way to get all you want is to help others get what they want. Serves without expecting anything in return. Very transformational in orientation. Value first orientation.
	Trait 14 – WORKING WITH OTHERS	
Finds it difficult to work with others. Struggles with giving others credit and wants to always be the star. Doesn't understand how to leverage other people's talent for value creation.	1 2 3 4 5 6 7 8 9 10	Works very well with others. Collaborates easily, doesn't mind who takes the credit as long as there are results. Understands how to leverage other people's talent to create value for all and capture value in return.
	Trait 15 – RELATIONSHIP WITH TIME	
Has little or no respect for time, theirs and others. Uses time accidentally, not intentionally. Has no daily plan for their use of time. Approaches each day as it comes. Always does what they want and ultimately not able to do what they have to do to get the results they desire in their lives. Values money more than time.	1 2 3 4 5 6 7 8 9 10	Has respect for time, theirs and others. Uses of time is deliberate, not accidental. Has a daily plan for their lives and works consistently towards their desired outcomes daily. Always does what they have to do so they can ultimately do what they want to do. Knows that time is more valuable than money.

Low									High
Trait 16 – RELATIONSHIP WITH THE FUTURE									
Short distance runners in their orientation; thinks and acts short term. The future is fuzzy at best, and they are unclear about how the actions they take today affects their future. Lack the discipline to delay gratification in the short term to enjoy a bright and exciting future. Have no clear vision of their future.	1	2	3	4	5	6	7	8	9	10	Long distance runners in their orientation; thinks long term, has a clear view of the future they are working towards and takes daily action with focus on their vision of the future. Can consistently delay gratification and exercise discipline in the short to medium term to enable them to achieve their future vision.
Trait 17 – RELATIONSHIP WITH MONEY									
Has poor, appalling relationship with money. Spends everything they have believing erroneously that they will save when they have more money. Very careless, even unintelligent in their money habit. Are not conscious of Proverbs 21 vs 20 and easily fall victim repeatedly.	1	2	3	4	5	6	7	8	9	10	Has exceptional relationship with money. Understands fundamentally that it is not how much money you make but how much you are able to keep, that matters. Knows that money is important and must be treated with care. Know Proverbs 21 vs 20 is real.
Trait 18 – ABILITY TO FOCUS									
Completely lacks focus and are forever chasing shiny objects or the latest ideas. Spreads themselves and their finite resources thin and engages in the 'undisciplined pursuit of more.' Have so many half-built bridges in their life and struggles to achieve meaningful success in anything.	1	2	3	4	5	6	7	8	9	10	Can Follow One Course Until Successful (FOCUS). Understands that resources are finite, hence the need to prioritise their activities and focus their resources on their most important opportunities. Engages in disciplined pursuit of less, knows that one fully built bridge is more important than a thousand half-built bridges.

	Low	High

Trait 19 – PROBLEM SOLVING

Problem identifier in orientation. Does not understand the success equation: BMP = BMO. Identifies problem, avoids them, and then complains they are not getting the breaks they need in life. Believes others should solve problems and do not take ownership for solving problems they encounter, thereby missing out on great opportunities.	1 2 3 4 5 6 7 8 9 10	Problem solver in orientation. Understands the success equation: BMP = BMO. Identifies problems, goes out of their way to solve it, thereby creating wealth for themselves and others. When they encounter problems, they say, "I Own This!" Knows the world rewards problem solvers and the number of problems they solve determines the amount of result they get.

Trait 20 – PAYING THE PRICE/SACRIFICE

Has a mentality of wanting something for nothing which always produces bad results in their lives. Always trying to look for shortcuts and avoids paying the right price for what they want. Always looking for free lunches and believes the world owes them.	1 2 3 4 5 6 7 8 9 10	Knows that there is a price for everything in life, you always must give something to get something. Understands that whatever they want in life that they don't yet have, is because they have not yet paid the price for having it. Knows that there is no free lunch.

Trait 21 – CONFRONTING REALITY

Either unwilling to or lacks the emotional fortitude to truly confront their brutal reality. Perpetually in self-denial, blaming everything & everyone on the outside for all their troubles. It is never their fault when things do not work out. Prefers people who will tell them what they want to hear and not the truth.	1 2 3 4 5 6 7 8 9 10	Consistent in their quest for the truth, the whole truth and nothing but the truth. Brutal in their assessment of their reality. Takes personal responsibility and knows that they are more guilty of self-sabotage than anything anyone is doing on the outside. Will rather have people around them tell them the truth especially about their blind spots.

Scoring Guide

> 126: **Excellent score.**

Continue a disciplined approach to improving your ownership index. Work on strengthening your lowest scoring items. Be committed to ongoing, continuous, and never-ending improvements. Consistency is crucial.

64 – 125: **Average score.**

Work in progress. Intentional actions are required to significantly improve behavior. Create an improvement plan and find an accountability partner to hold you accountable for the level of progress made.

< 63: **Serious work required.**

Consider declaring a state of emergency on your personal growth and development. Look for coaches and mentors. Take deliberate actions towards overhauling your ownership behavior. Do whatever it takes to improve. And do it as quickly as possible.

CHAPTER 2

THE GIFT OF INSPIRATION

*"At any given moment, you have the power to say:
'This is not how the story is going to end."*
- Christine Miller

The lessons I am about to share with you in this personal story have the potential to transform your life. It is often said that the greatest gift you can give anyone is the gift of inspiration. If this is true, and I believe it is, then the greatest gift you can ever receive from anyone is the gift of inspiration. So many people miss this important point to their huge disadvantage. *Some of the people in your life are there to inspire you and not to meet your needs.* It is so important that you recognize this. If you are blind to this, you will miss out on the greatest gift they can give you, because you will focus on the material things that you can get from them or on their shortcomings.

I have been blessed to have had many opportunities to be inspired, and I can tell you first-hand that it is one of the most beautiful experiences anyone can have. My life has been so profoundly transformed by certain moments of inspiration that I now engage in the deliberate act of looking for inspiration daily. I strongly recommend that you do the same.

Before I go into the life transforming story I promised to share, let us consider for a moment exactly what it means to be inspired. The Collins Dictionary defines inspiration as "a feeling of enthusiasm you get from someone or something, which gives you new and creative ideas." If I were to personally define inspiration, I would describe it as a powerful moment of awakening. A freeze in time when you are acutely aware of a creative idea, your creative potential, and the sheer magnitude of your capabilities. In those moments, a person can conquer the unconquerable because the force of faith is let loose. When you are inspired, there are no boundaries in your mind, no chains on your thoughts, no barriers, and no barricades. All that you see are possibilities. Moments of inspiration always leave you awakened and stimulated to achieve great things. I dare say that an inspiration a day will do more for your future success than anything else you can imagine.

Inspiration can come in different forms and can be pleasant or unpleasant. Whatever form or shape it comes in is irrelevant; what is important is how you respond to it.

In fact, I have found that the sources of inspiration that have fueled my greatest achievements have not stemmed from a place of 'ease and quiet'. Rather, they have been born from a place of great need—the need to survive, the need to thrive, and the need to be victorious when confronted with difficult circumstances.

The Gift of Inspiration that Changed my Life

By far, one of the greatest inspirations I have ever received came from a prospective client. The incident itself was a very unpleasant experience, and many people would have reacted badly to it. However, for me, it proved life changing, and luckily for me, it happened very early in my entrepreneurial journey. If it had happened much later than it did, I probably would not have been in the position to write this book.

It so happened that one of my colleagues succeeded in securing a high-value meeting with the CEO of an indigenous and very successful company. For months, we had been working hard and seeking for an opportunity to acquire this company as a client. And so, when we received the news that we had secured a meeting with the CEO, we were all super excited and hopeful that our breakthrough moment with the company had finally arrived.

On the day of the meeting with the CEO, three of my colleagues and I packed ourselves into my beat-up car and headed to the venue armed with one of the most rehearsed PowerPoint presentations on Business Growth Strategy ever put together in the history of PowerPoint! We had spent the previous three days researching and creating this presentation because we were determined to land this very important client. And although we did not know it at the time, that even though the meeting would end without us winning the business, it would end with me winning one of the best gifts I have ever received as an entrepreneur till date.

Upon arriving at the meeting venue, the security guard directed us to park in the CEO's visitors' carport. I felt a bit uneasy about this, especially after seeing the other cars that were parked in this space. Let's just say that parking my car there would completely change the landscape—the look and feel of the entire parking lot.

Unfortunately for us, the security man insisted that it was the only space available, so we ended up parking in the allocated spot. Little did we know that the CEO's CCTV coverage included that parking space, and he witnessed everything about our arrival.

After reluctantly parking there, we were ushered into the boardroom, and offered tea with biscuits. I was too nervous to eat or drink anything at that point, so we set up our presentation and waited for the CEO to join us.

He came into the boardroom right on time, and we stood up as he greeted us warmly and asked what he could do for us. I introduced our firm as a Business Strategy and HR Consulting firm and told him that we came prepared to present our *Business Growth and Effectiveness Strategy* solution to his company.

He smiled, and I could have sworn that I saw a bit of amusement behind that smile.

Anyway, he asked us to proceed, and we went on to deliver one of the best pitching presentations we had ever given until that point. It took us about 55-60 minutes to go through our almost 70 slides. He sat through it all rather patiently, nodded at intervals, and asked a couple of questions for clarification. He even jotted down a couple of notes on his notepad, an act that encouraged us to pitch even more.

When we were done, he congratulated us on the outstanding presentation, saying he was impressed with the presentation's quality and depth.

Then he delivered perhaps the greatest gift I have received in business to date. Even though this event took place about 15 years ago, I still remember his comments vividly as if they were only delivered to me yesterday.

He asked us if we wanted an honest or diplomatic feedback. I felt the muscle in my stomach tightening and blood draining from my face. It was as if I knew what was coming.

I replied in a weak voice and with a nervous smile, ''Brutally honest feedback, sir.''

He smiled, sat up from his chair and delivered the most inspiring feedback I have ever heard.

"Guys, I am confused," he began. "I have listened to your presentation, and it is top quality. Clearly, you guys know your stuff, at least theoretically. But here is my challenge: If you know this much about Business Strategy and Growth, why don't you practice it on your business first? Prove that it works before trying to sell it to others."

At this point he paused for some seconds, as if to let his point sink home for us. And then he continued, "I saw you drive in earlier today, and no disrespect, but none of our employees will be allowed to drive such a car. But here you are with all your knowledge of Strategy and Growth, and you can't seem to apply it to your own business.

"If you had driven in here with a decent car or cars, and I am not saying it must be flashy, or anything like that, decent is good enough, and you gave this sort of presentation, I will be crazy not to want to do business with you. I am a pragmatic business owner, and I know for a fact that charity begins at home. I want to work with people that are 'eating their own cooking'".

He then went on to give us this timeless advice:

"If I were you, I would spend time applying this to my business. First, prove that it works and then go out and help others. This is my feedback to you.

"If I give you any business today, I will be doing you guys a disservice, and chances are you won't learn this crucial lesson. **You cannot give what you don't have!**

"If such a time comes when you can prove to me that you have successfully applied what you are selling to your business, I promise to give you audience. But for now, you guys have a lot of work to do internally first. This should be your most important project of all."

Wow! Wow!! Wow!!!

I was completely blown away. It felt as if I was having an out-of-body experience, like I was floating. Up until that point, it had never crossed my mind to think, really think, about applying the exact principles we were learning to our business. At least, not in the way he had recommended.

From the core of my being, I knew at that very moment that things could never remain the same again. Never!

We thanked him for his feedback, quickly made our way out of the boardroom and back to our car. As soon as we got to the car, as I recall, one of my colleagues' reaction to the CEO's feedback was saying that the man was very arrogant. I told him that I completely disagreed with him. I also told him that the feedback we had just received was a gift and that what we did with it mattered more than anything else.

There and then, I had a strong impression in my soul that I had just had a destiny-shaping encounter. One that I must never allow to slip out of my mind. One that if I held desperately on to, and leveraged, would completely revolutionize my approach to my business and to my life. Without any doubt in my mind, I knew that I was not permitted to ever forget that lesson! And I hope you always remember that lesson too.

As we drove out of the company, I looked back and said two things to myself.

First, I bear no grudge in my mind towards this person. Instead, I admire and bless him in my heart for taking a chance to be brutally honest with us. His feedback was indeed a gift that I will cherish forever. He could have just said that he would get back to us and move on (which is exactly what most people would do). So, I really appreciated the fact that he went out of his way to give us the feedback.

Second, I said to myself, "I'll be back, bigger and better. I'll pay the price, whatever it is (excluding sin and crime). And next time, I will prove that I have applied what I know to my life and to my business and I will have the external manifestation to prove it."

And I did.

I took the gift and went to work. I went about relentlessly applying what I had learnt, first to my business. And this has been the difference that made a significant difference.

Fast forward to about ten years later, we organized a conference in the 750-seater hall in our new Conference Centre, and we invited the co-founder of that CEO's company to be the keynote speaker.

I had originally wanted to invite the other founder who had inspired me years earlier. But he was out of the country, and we had to settle for his co-founder.

He was introduced to me by one of my business directors as he took a seat beside me. After his keynote address, he congratulated me on the amazing structure and quality of our facility as well as the successful execution of our conference.

Then, he asked the magic question, "Can I please have your phone number?"

I said, "Sure, it will be my pleasure, sir," as I smiled quietly on the outside.

But on the inside, I screamed YES!!! I could not stop smiling for weeks after that encounter.

So, I ask you these questions. *What is your source of inspiration?* What or who inspires you to the heights of productivity? How do you seek inspiration? Are you even deliberate about seeking inspiration?

Without inspiration, you can only go so far. Inspiration is a catalyst that pushes you to achieve great things.

I encourage you to go all out in looking for inspiration. And when you do find it, make the most of it.

Key Takeaways

- The greatest gift you can ever receive from anyone is the gift of inspiration.

- It is important to recognize that some of the people in your life are there to inspire you and not to meet your needs. If you don't, you will miss out on the greatest gift they can give you, because you will focus on the material things that you can get from them or on their shortcomings.

- Inspiration can come in different forms; they can be pleasant or unpleasant. Wherever or whatever form or shape it comes in is irrelevant; what is important is how you react to it.

- The sources of inspiration that have fueled my greatest achievements have not stemmed from a place of 'ease and quiet'. Rather, they have been born from a place of great need; the need to survive, the need to thrive, and the need to be victorious when confronted with difficult circumstances.

- Identify your sources of inspiration and seek daily inspiration. Without inspiration, you can only go so far. Inspiration is a catalyst that pushes you to achieve great things.

CHAPTER 3

THE ULTIMATE WISDOM PRINCIPLE

"Every dream has a process and a price tag. Those who embrace the process and pay the price, live the dream. Those who don't, just dream."

- Jeremy Riddle

A powerful king once called his wise men together and directed them to prepare a compilation of all the wisdom in the world and bring their findings to him. This was to fulfil his ambition of becoming the wisest king that ever lived.

The wise men worked for several months, frantically researching, and discussing a wide variety of subjects. Finally, they presented the king with ten volumes of information that they were confident would certainly please him.

The king perused a few pages of one volume, then said, "This is far too much material. Surely you can give me the wisdom of the world in less than ten volumes." So, the king sent his wise men back to summarize the wisdom contained in their ten volumes. It took many more months, but they had reduced their findings to a single volume when they were done.

Feeling even more confident than the first time, the wise men handed the king their work, at which point he again perused a few pages. Shaking his head with dissatisfaction, he looked up and said, "Still far too much. I have no intention of reading all these materials. Do you know how many wives I must care for? Surely the wisdom of the world can be reduced to less than one volume."

The wise men, frustrated by the king's latest request, decided to go to the extreme and reduce their findings to one page. This took them several months, and this time around, they were very pleased with their output feeling confident that the king would surely now be happy.

To their utter amazement, however, he was not. "Still too much material," bellowed the king. "What I want is the wisdom of the world summarized in one sentence," he finally clarified. The wise men gulped in dismay. How were they supposed to do that, they wanted to ask, but dared not for fear of losing their heads, literally? How could all the wisdom of the world possibly be reduced to a single sentence?

The only positive thing about this seemingly impossible task was that they knew that it would mark the end of the matter. They had two options: succeed in giving the king what he wanted—the wisdom of the world summarized in one sentence or be prepared to answer a very angry king. To say the least, the task proved to be daunting. However, after considerable reflection and debate, they finally succeeded in condensing all their findings into a single sentence.

Proudly but fearfully, they approached the throne and said to the king, "Your majesty, we have at last summarized all the wisdom of the world in one sentence". After that, the wisest of the wise men handed the king a single sheet of parchment and quickly stepped back, waiting for his fate and those of his fellow wise men. The king looked at the parchment and smiled, nodding his head approvingly. "This surely is the greatest wisdom of the world", he said, congratulating the wise men.

Then he read the sentence aloud: *THERE IS NO FREE LUNCH!*

This, my friend, is the ultimate wisdom principle. There is no free lunch! **If you want to succeed in life, you must be willing to pay the price for that success.**

This holds true in every facet of our lives, and most of all, in our professional lives. For instance, a professional that must wake up by 4 am daily to ensure that he beats the early morning traffic, trades off a few hours of essential sleep time to secure his source of income. A C-suite executive that leads her industry or organization, trades off massive amounts of resources (time, energy, and money) to acquire the cutting-edge know-how that keeps her ahead of her other professional colleagues in her industry or organization.

If you think about it carefully, you too have made hundreds of trade-offs to get to where you currently are in your career. In the same way, if you will succeed in creating the wealth you need to own your future, you must necessarily make even more trade-offs to actualize that goal. It is non-negotiable.

Sooner or later (hopefully sooner), we all learn this truth and come to understand that *there is a price for everything in life.* There is a price for taking the right action, there is a price for taking the wrong action, and yes, there is a price for taking no action at all. You must always give something up to get something in return.

Since this seems so simple, why do people still get stuck?

Empirical evidence suggests that even though most adults understand this principle at an intellectual (head) level, they do not accept it on an emotional (heart) level. Their knowledge of this fundamental principle hardly translates into action, resulting in a mentality of wanting something for nothing which always produces terrible consequences. This category of people earnestly search for *Easy Street.* They would rather wait endlessly for the elevator than take the stairs. Unfortunately, they have programmed their brains to always seek out the easier route.

All too frequently, people settle for less because the alternative appears too stressful. They quit exercise and diets because they feel they are too hard. They stop advancing in their careers and in their lives because it seems like too much work. They do not want to work for bosses who are too tough and demanding. They cannot deal with being uncomfortable, so they seek the shortcut, and when they can't find it, they quit. They are not willing to sacrifice and pay the price.

If by any means you once belonged or belong to this category of individuals, but you have come to the inevitable realization that such thinking only leads to a dead end, and yet you simply do not know how to consistently get yourself to do the difficult things that bring success, let me share a secret with you about how to tackle hard things.

How to do the Hard Things that Bring Success

To tackle hard things, do something harder first! It is called the **hardest-first technique**.

One of Muhammed Ali's most famous sayings is, "The fight is won or lost far away from witnesses – behind the lines, in the gym, and out there on the road, long before I dance under those lights."

It is said that the great boxer used a method similar to the hardest-first technique in preparing for his fights. In choosing his boxing workout partners, he would make sure that the practice partners he worked with before a fight were tougher than the boxer he was going up against in the real fight. He went out of his way to find multiple practice partners who were each better than his upcoming opponent in one way or another. After facing these practice partners, he went into his real fight with an air of confidence that he had already tackled his opponent's strengths and had won.

I strongly recommend this technique to you. Whenever you are faced with a hard but necessary task, set up a tougher battle than the one you must face. If you have something hard to do and you are hesitant to do it, pick out something even harder and do that first. For instance, if you must make a sales call to someone who scares you, you should find a way to rehearse it first in front of someone who scares you more, for example, your boss. If you try it, you will find that it does wonders for your confidence and motivation when you go into the real situation.

Remember, the harder you are on yourself, the easier life is on you. The more you sweat in peace time, the less you bleed in war.

Success requires sacrifice, discomfort and even pain sometimes. This is because the things that make people successful, are the hard things that everyone else tries to hide from.

So, ask yourself this question truthfully: **What would I have to sacrifice to have what I really, really want?** My hours of mindless TV watching, my social life, time with friends, my free time, or the number of hours I sleep?

Now answer this question: **What am I willing to sacrifice?**

If these two lists do not match up, you simply do not want that success badly enough.

And if you are okay with just getting by, I want to ask you why. If you are not willing to put in the hard work and the commitment, I would like to know why.

What are you saving yourself for? Why are you not giving life your best shot? Why are you not living up to your full potentials?

For some people, being average is enough. And I am not judging. They neither want the pressure nor the stress, nor having to sacrifice time with friends and family. Instead, they want to party when the mood strikes, sleep late whenever they can, and get up and go to bed with little worries, responsibilities, and pressure. I get that. It is a much easier way to experience life.

However, people with this approach to life are the same people who look around at others who are more successful and say things like, "I can't believe how lucky that guy is, or that person must be up to something shady or that person must be fronting for someone else."

Do not be jealous of someone who succeeds, especially if you had the same opportunities and refused to make the most of them. Stop justifying your lack of willingness to pay the price by diminishing other people's accomplishments. Like they say, if you can't take the heat, stay out of the kitchen.

One of the most profound philosophies you can develop in life is accepting that there is no free lunch. You must be ready and willing to always pay the price for whatever you want.

The question is, ***will you pay the right price to get what you want in life?***

Key Takeaways

- The ultimate wisdom principle is that there is no free lunch! If you want to succeed in life, you must be willing to pay the price for that success. You must give something up to get something in return.

- Empirical evidence suggests that even though most adults understand this principle at an intellectual level, they do not accept it on an emotional level. Many people settle for less because the price for success is high. They quit doing the right things because it feels hard, which is why people get stuck.

- To tackle hard things, do something harder first! It's called the *hardest-first technique*.

- The harder you are on yourself, the easier life is on you. The more you sweat in peacetime, the less you bleed in war.

- What do you have to sacrifice to get what you really want? Could it be hours of mindless TV watching, excessive social life, your free time, or the number of hours you sleep? Are you willing to make the sacrifice?

CHAPTER 4

HOW TO BECOME MORE VALUABLE IN LIFE, CAREER, AND BUSINESS

"Strive not to be a success, but rather to be of value."

- Albert Einstein

In a world that is saturated with distractions, it is vital to live with the consciousness that your attention is constantly being contested for, and, in the words of Winston Churchill, "if you stop and throw stones at every dog that barks, you will never reach your destination." Especially if that destination or goal is to be successful in your life, your career, or your business.

Distraction is a 21st century plague. It threatens every one of us. To keep myself from being derailed and submerged under the avalanche of reasonable and unreasonable distractions, every morning, and early too, I program my mind and my day by asking myself this powerful question:

How do I become more valuable and get more of what I want in life?

If you desire to live a life of significance, this question is one that you MUST ask yourself, preferably daily. I have met way too many people who desire much more from life than they are currently getting. Their hearts are full of big dreams and impressive plans. Unfortunately, that is pretty much where it all stops—at the level of dreams. They mistakenly believe that if they wished harder, their desires would materialize, and all that they want would manifest.

They go with the flow every day, paying no attention to the significance of every minute, every hour, and every day. Rather than taking calculated steps towards the actualization of their goals, they spend considerable periods of time 'willing' the manifestation of their desires, claiming to deploy the Law of Attraction. Unfortunately, this never gets anyone very far, if at all it gets them anywhere. Focusing exclusively on what you want or need without having an accurate roadmap to actualize those goals and desires is the reason why many people end up dispirited and frustrated with their circumstances. Life simply does not work that way.

The secret to getting more in life (legitimately) is to make yourself worth more.

This is because how much value you can create will determine how much value you can capture. And if you go a step further by creating value that is so unique and so differentiated that you stand in a class all on your own, then the sky literally becomes the starting point for how much value you can have.

Becoming More Valuable

So, the big question is: *How do you go about making yourself worth more?*

Here is a step-by-step process that has worked for me over time, and I am confident that it will work for you too.

Step 1:
You must start by finding out what your target audience wants or what they need to be successful.

Your target audience could be employers (if you are looking for a job), clients (if you are looking for business), congregation (if you are a pastor), voters (if you are a politician), etc. Since you will not be serving yourself, your quest to become more valuable must start with your target audience: the people you must create value for.

Your focus should be on what will make them succeed, excel, shine, grow, improve, raise their game, change direction, climb to the top, become better, etc. Focusing on your own wants and needs will not get you anywhere. You must focus disproportionately on what your target audience wants or needs. This is the starting point of the value creation and capture process. It is such an obvious principle, and yet it is one that is grossly overlooked.

To help you get started in the right direction, here are some of the questions you can ask your target audience to discover what they truly want.

- What are you struggling with?

- What is your team struggling with?

- What questions do you wish you had more or better answers to?

- What is your number one question about *XYZ*?

- What is the one thing that will have a domino effect and make all the difference if you have it or get it right?

I call this the *Problem Identification* Phase of the Becoming More Valuable process.

Step 2:
After identifying what your target audience needs, you must go and get it for them.

Every successful business executes this single step correctly every single day, they make something that people want or need. There is nothing more valuable than being able to recognize and meet an unmet need. This is the stuff millionaires are made of. Millionaires are simply people that meet a nagging need of over a million people. So, if you have clarity on what your target audience wants, and you have taken the time to validate that it will help them succeed, your next assignment is to go and get it for them.

This is referred to as the *Solution Design and Development* Phase. It is the process of creating, developing, or building the things people need. Where possible, it is best to co-create it with the target audience, and pilot test the solution with some of your target audience for further validation.

During this stage, it is supremely vital to understand that there are two broad categories of solutions you can potentially offer: The vitamin-based solutions, and the painkiller-based solutions.

Whenever people come to me to sell a business idea or concept, the first thing I want to know is if what they are proposing to sell is a vitamin or a painkiller. Viewing your business idea through this lens is a crucial way to avoid building a service or product that only a few people want, or worse, one that no one wants or needs.

The fact is that everyone recognizes that vitamins are good for them, but most people only remember to take their vitamins occasionally. Like actual vitamins, vitamin-based solutions are seen as 'nice to have,' but not 'essential to have.' They are services or products that are considered optional, and because people make decisions based on intense need, vitamin-based solutions sell slowly, if at all.

On the other hand, unlike vitamins, painkillers are not 'nice to have', they are urgent necessities. Painkillers give immediate relief from pain. People hate pain and will go to extreme lengths to stop it. Therefore, if you can identify a pain point that is shared by a lot of people and you are able to design an effective solution to that problem, you have struck gold!

Note, however, that the powerful insights that enable the creation of a product that meets the criteria of a painkiller do not come from sitting at your desk and brainstorming ideas. It comes from interacting with your target audience to deeply study and understand their needs. Steve Jobs told us Apple's secret of success when he said, "Get closer than ever to your customers. So close that you tell them what they need well before they realize it themselves."

Every product or service is either a vitamin or a painkiller. Painkillers sell faster. That's just the way it is. Therefore, when starting a business, it is critical to take the time to research and find an accurate answer to the question of whether what you are creating is a vitamin or a painkiller. This detail matters, and it is worth waiting to get it right at the beginning.

So, what business solution are you currently contemplating? Is it a vitamin or a painkiller?

Always remember this fact, individuals and businesses learn to live with certain things. They develop coping mechanisms. They become accustomed to their issues, challenges, or problems and hence develop inertia that makes taking actions to change difficult.

If you are planning to develop a solution that solves your target audience's problems, to avoid the 'landmine' of creating solutions that people do not really want or need, make sure the problem you are trying to solve ticks the following boxes:

- Does the problem require a painkiller or a vitamin type intervention?
- Is the problem urgent in nature?
- Is the problem pervasive?
- Are people willing to pay to solve it?

If the problem you are aiming to solve does not tick these boxes, be warned that going ahead might end in frustration for both you and your target audience.

I call this the *Solution Development* Phase in the Becoming More Valuable process.

Step 3:
After creating the solution your target audience needs, you must give it to them in a compelling way.

People are not interested in what you are selling. *People are interested in what your product or solution can do for them.* In other words, they are interested in *transformation.*

For transformation to take place, it is important to create the right experiences for your target audience. You must deliver the value you offer in a unique and compelling way to differentiate you from your rivals. You must deliver it with style.

I once read the story of a carpenter who grew from a one-man shop into a massive furniture company with multiple branches, by practising the principle of 'going the extra mile.' Anytime he got an order to produce a piece of furniture, be it a cupboard, desk, chair, table, etc., not only did he make the best quality product possible, but he also always went out of his way to make something extra that was of value to his clients. He created handy items like piggy banks, small stools, wooden combs, or chopping boards, using the leftover materials. Soon, his reputation grew, and before long, he became a major furniture manufacturer.

This anecdote tells a significant truth. One of the most potent and underutilized principles of success is developing the habit of going the extra mile. One writer aptly said, "The man who does more than he is paid for will soon be paid for more than he does." So, make it a practice to go the extra mile and opportunities will follow you everywhere. It is a universal law.

Remember to always give more than you expect to get in return. Always. Be the 'Carpenter' in your career, business, vocation, etc. It can be the difference that makes a difference.

I call this the *Solution Delivery* Phase of the *Becoming More Valuable* process.

Step 4:
You must do Steps 1, 2 & 3 all over again.

It is essential to make this your default operating model and to do it continuously if you desire to become more valuable. The more you do this, the better you get at it; the better you get, the more value you will create; the more value you create, the more value you can capture for yourself, and the more value you capture, the more valuable you become. Consistency is key.

During this process, **you MUST concentrate on quality, service and delivering results first,** and the reward will follow naturally as a result. Do this consistently and you can never lose in the long run.

This is what I refer to as *the Value Creation Process Mastery* Phase.

If you want more, then make yourself worth more. You must be committed to the process of value creation if you want to become more valuable. Practicing steps 1 - 4 above consistently will take you very far in life.

Key Takeaways

- Distraction is a 21st century plague. To keep yourself from getting derailed in your quest for success, start off every day by asking and answering this question: *How do I become more valuable and get more of what I want in life?*

- The secret to getting more in life is to make yourself worth more because how much value you create determines how much value you can capture.

- To make yourself worth more, take these four steps:

- Step 1: Start by finding out what your target audience wants or needs to be successful.

- Step 2: After identifying what your target audience needs, get it for them.

- All products and services fall into two categories: they are either vitamins (nice-to-haves) or painkillers (must-haves). Painkillers sell faster. Build products and services that are painkillers.

- Step 3: After creating the solution your target audience needs, you must give it to them in a compelling way.

- Step 4: To remain valuable repeat steps 1, 2 & 3 again and again.

CHAPTER 5

THE MAGIC OF GOAL SETTING

"Without goals and plans to reach them, you are like a ship that has set sail with no destination."
- Fitzhugh Dodson

Have you heard the advice that what you do not know cannot hurt you? Well, that is a terribly bad piece of advice! What you do not know can not only hurt you, but it can also have devastating impact on the people closest to you, including your future. Of all the things that you do not know that can hurt you very badly, the critically important knowledge of setting goals and following through with them ranks at the very top.

Not having goals and trying to navigate your life, business or career is akin to a hunter going into the forest to hunt and firing his arrow or gun indiscriminately in the hope that a deer will accidentally run into one of his bullets. This is probably the worst strategy anyone can adopt for living. Unfortunately, most people are guilty of living their lives without setting goals.

You may wonder why people fail to set goals for their lives? I strongly believe that there are two major reasons. First, many people do not appreciate the sheer power that setting and achieving goals brings into their lives. And second, even for those that know a thing or two about the importance of goal setting, that knowledge benefits them very little because they do not know how to correctly set the right goals.

The good news is that this is about to change. This chapter is dedicated to the best Goal Setting Framework in the World—the *10 F's of Goal Setting*. Why is it the best in the world you ask? Well, for one thing, it can help you achieve everything you want, literally. And you should know by now that I would not say such a thing flippantly.

What is the greatest accomplishment of mankind?

Some say it is walking on the moon. Others say it is the development of vaccines. Still others say that it is the declaration of human rights. While the list can go on indefinitely, one thing is certain, whatever takes the title of the greatest accomplishment of mankind was once a dream. It was likely the dream of one person, then it became the goal of a group of people, and finally they achieved it. So, when I say that goal setting has the power to bring your best dreams to life, give you everything you desire and help you live a well-balanced life, it is neither an exaggeration nor an overstatement. Everything is literally possible when there is a well set up and defined goal, the willpower to succeed, and the faith to persevere.

Anyone can 'goal-set' their way to their highest dreams

There are two things that I believe everyone desires. One, to see all their dreams come true, and, two, to have a balanced life while bringing these dreams to pass. I am no different. But like many people today, several years ago, all I had were my dreams and little else in terms of the mechanisms required to fulfil those dreams. I would say that all of that changed when I listened to an audio tape on goal setting by Jim Rohn. Let's just say that many of the things Jim Rohn said turned my world upside down, transformed me into a goal setting machine and made me a man that has seen many big dreams come true.

Naturally, my goal setting successes have changed me into the type of person that sets weekly, monthly, quarterly, half year and yearly goals, 3 to 5-year goals, and even 10 to 15-year goals. I am so committed to goal setting that when I am planning for a new year, it is almost as if I am going into war. I take time to think deeply about what I want, asking myself about what I would like to accomplish. If there is anything that has made the difference in the outcome of my life till date, goal setting is it. Knowing how to set and achieve goals has so radically altered my life's results that when I see people trivializing this powerful practice, I feel deeply saddened for them. It is like watching a man with a goldmine in his backyard roaming about broke and disillusioned. The Holy Bible says something that always puts me on my toes. "People perish for a lack of knowledge." How true.

If you take nothing away from this entire book, I truly hope that some of my passion for goal setting rubs off on you. If you can catch this goal setting bug that I am trying to pass on to you, I promise that it will prove to be the solution that you have been craving for. If I was not convinced that the practice of setting and achieving goals would create the kind of circumstances that you desire, I would not write this chapter, neither will there be hundreds, if not thousands of books, and millions of articles written on the potency of goal setting.

Goal Setting for Balance

When I first started setting goals, I was totally consumed with the goal of building my business. As I began to gradually achieve that goal, I found that something was wrong. With all my energies focused on building my business, I found that my goal setting framework left me trading one dream for another. As my business grew, some aspects of my personal life were taking a bad hit. This compelled me to search for a goal setting framework that enabled me achieve balance in all areas of my life. After trying many different frameworks, I finally developed what I honestly consider to be the most effective goal setting framework I have ever used or come across. I am convinced that the framework has proven to be very effective because I incorporated the best features from all the other frameworks I had previously used. And I adjusted the framework to suit my needs—the greatest of which had become the need to achieve balance in my life. Before I get into the nuts and bolts of my goal setting framework, it is crucial that I first expound on the foundational principle behind the need to achieve a balanced and well-adjusted life.

A Life Balance Test

One of God's best gifts to mankind is the gift of the imagination. And I love to use my gift quite often. I have imagined my life all the way to the end. I have imagined how all the key aspects of my life will turn out. I have imagined how my family, business associates and friends will gather to celebrate what will be considered as a well-lived and well-utilized life when my days on earth are complete. I have imagined what each person will say about me, how they will recall that I had been a great father, friend, spouse, associate, boss, and the world's greatest granddad. It is with these pleasant imaginations that I set my life goals. It is with them that I order my actions day by day, month by month, and year by year to chart the course of my entire destiny.

So far, the result of this intentional living has been inspirational and truly life transforming for me. It makes me excited to wake up in the morning, and it makes me tap dance all the way to work. As impressive as this style of living may appear, I did not arrive at it by being the wisest guy on the block. It arose from a place of discontentment with the imbalances in my life. There were multiple triggers, alarm bells if you will, that alerted me to the fact that I was leaving too much to chance and not taking better charge of all the aspects of my life. One of such triggers was the Life Balance Assessment Test, (popularly known as *the Wheel of Life*) that I had the good fortune of taking several years back.

The Wheel of Life is powerful because it gives you a striking visual representation of your life as it currently is, compared with the way you would like it to be. It is called the 'Wheel of Life' because each area of your life is mapped on a circle, like the spokes of a wheel. The concept was originally created by Paul J. Meyer, founder of Success Motivation® Institute, Inc.

And I would like you to take the test. Doing so will enable you to examine your life as a whole. It will give you an immediate 'helicopter' overview of your current life balance, so that you have a good idea of how balanced or bumpy your life is. By taking time to evaluate your satisfaction with all the critical facets of your life, you will see where you are out of balance and where you have great satisfaction. The test will help you determine where you want to focus your goal setting energies in the future—areas that are strong that you would like to enhance, as well as developing areas that you need to do better in.

Taking the test will start you on the journey to following Jack Welch's advice when he said, "Control your own destiny or someone else will."

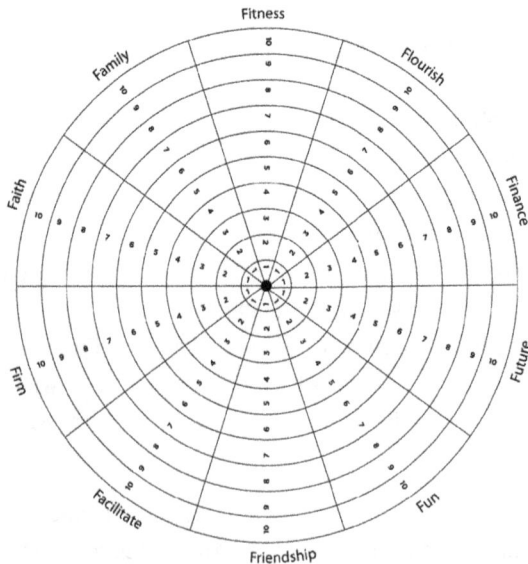

Figure 2: The Wheel of Life

How to take the Wheel of Life Assessment

Simply use the scale of 0 – 10 to plot your level of satisfaction with each section of your life, with 10 being extreme satisfaction and 0 being extreme dissatisfaction. On the wheel, indicate the number that best expresses your level of satisfaction with each section of your life with a dot. After you have dotted all the sections of the wheel, join all the dots to form an unbroken ring.

Figure 3 is an example of a completed wheel. Yours could be more balanced or bumpier, the aesthetics do not matter. What counts is that you are objective and open-minded about the exercise to enable you get a true picture of the current state of your affairs.

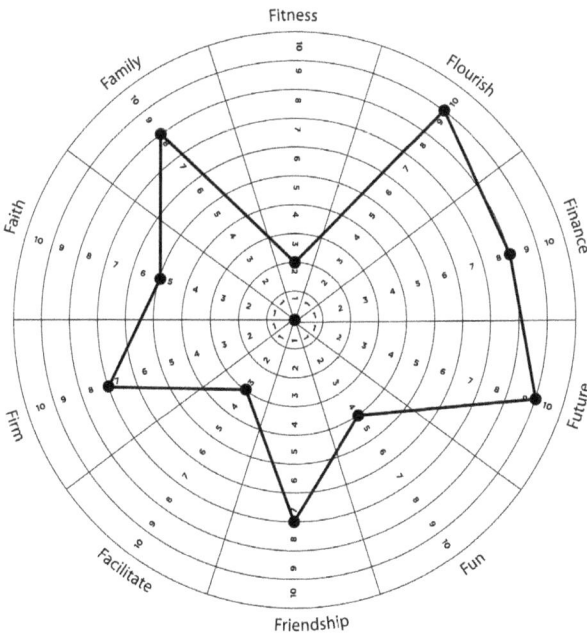

Figure 3: A Charted Wheel of Life

Now that you have a visual on how all the various aspects of your life look, if you were to travel on a long journey with wheels shaped like that, would your experience be smooth, rough, or even dangerous? What word pops up in your mind when you see your wheel? If someone offered you a ride in a car with wheels shaped like this, would you happily accept the ride?

The Wheel of Life exercise is very revealing and sobering. When I first took it, it revealed all my blind spots and the areas where I needed to make major improvements to support myself and my loved ones. I have never looked back or backed down since that experience. It prompted the development of the *10-Fs Goal Setting Framework* that I have so far used to create a life that I love, one that I am proud of and one that has greatly benefited me and those that I love.

I am more than happy to share this framework with you in the hope that it helps you create a life that is balanced and productive all-round.

The 10 F's Personal Goal Setting Framework

Faith	Family	Fitness
Flourish	Finance	Firm
Facilitate	Friendship	Fun
Future		

The entire framework is built on what I consider to be the ten major pillars of a person's life, and its strength lies in the fact that it seeks to drive balance in all ten areas. Achieving balance is key to a long and strong life because every imbalance that we tolerate for a long time weakens another aspect of our lives that also matters. I have learnt the hard way to resist every form of imbalance in my life, because I have seen first-hand the damage that it can do to the future. I invite you to do the same by adopting this goal setting framework. Let's now run through each 'F', filling in the framework as you set goals with schedules and timelines for each of these 10 areas of your life.

Pillar 1: Faith

The framework starts with faith because if you are a person of faith, especially one that believes in a Higher Being (God), and you are living your life accordingly, it is your faith that encourages you, gives you inner strength and hope, and helps you in hard times. Faith has to do with your religion, beliefs, purpose, and reason for being. Personally, my entire life is anchored on my faith. Because of how critical faith is, it is something that you must keep on top of daily. An example of a goal for your faith could be to ensure that you attend worship sessions every week unfailingly. You could add to that praying twice a day and studying the Bible for 30 minutes daily. To deepen your faith-walk, you could set goals to meditate for 15 minutes or more daily. If you believe in going to confessions, you could set a goal to make your confessions every week. Whatever you consider as important to helping you grow your faith and giving you the strength to go through life must be put in the goal section for your faith and scheduled.

Pillar 2: Family

After tasting the heights of power and fame, Barbara Bush, the wife of the 41st President of America said, "When all the dust is settled, and all the crowds are gone, the things that matter are faith, family, and friends." The fact is that without family, there is really nothing worth working for or working towards. And yet sometimes, especially for businesspeople, there is a tendency to be so focused on work that their families take a back seat. There must be a way to balance business with family and the only way is to have a goal for family time.

Examples of family goals could be to have a movie night every Thursday or Friday or take the family for dinner outside the home. Schedule a special time with each family member to have heartfelt conversations that nurture deeper bonding. Whatever suits your context, just be sure that it is something structured and scheduled so that everyone looks forward to those times. If it is not done this way, it will never happen. Family goals must also include your extended family members as well. You must schedule time every week to call your parents and other relatives. Activities that ensure that you are keeping in touch with your family and staying on top of your responsibilities are very important.

Pillar 3: Fitness

Bret Contreras, a sports scientist, once said, "If you think lifting is dangerous, try being weak. Being weak is dangerous." Without health, there is no vehicle to pursue wealth, making goals in this area critically important. It is all too easy to get very busy, negligent, and overweight, which always creates problems in the future. I have seen these outcomes one too many times. There is a saying that at the early part of your life, if you use your health to pursue wealth, when you have attained wealth and your health has forsaken you, you will use your wealth to pursue health. But this does not have to be the case, and the only way to avoid health problems while we pursue success is to keep physical fitness goals. From establishing daily exercise routines that you can keep to, for instance, walking 5000 to 10,000 steps a day, eating healthily, and cutting out junk food, excess sugar, and oily foods. You need to keep your body healthy to live a truly balanced life.

Pillar 4: Flourish

"I constantly see people rise in life who are not the smartest, sometimes not even the most diligent, but they are learning machines. They go to bed every night a little wiser than they were when they got up and boy does that help, particularly when you have a long run ahead of you." Charles T. Munger said these words, and I literally live by them, so should anyone who will succeed and remain successful for a long time.

Flourish is all about your learning and personal development. *How do you intend to grow? What kind of investments do you want to make in yourself to make sure that you are learning more, growing more, and improving the probability of your success as an individual?* It is vital to have goals around things that will help you to flourish and succeed in life. A good example of flourish goals could be to read a set number of books every month, attend a pre-determined number of courses every year, identify mentors you wish to seek, connect with and gain from, coaches to hire, audio books to listen to, podcasts to digest, and so on. Whatever works for you and ensures that you are in a continuous, never-ending learning and development mode should be written down as your goals in this area. Bear in mind that what you capture in your flourish goals should be based on all that you know you need to learn to move to the next level in your life.

Pillar 5: Finance

Money is important, and anyone who thinks otherwise is either lying or deluded. While it is true that money is not everything, one thing is sure, without it, you cannot get anything in this world. Having more than just enough money means good schools for your kids, a roof over your head, food to eat, vacations to enjoy a beautiful life, etc. So, having goals that speak to and create clarity around how to keep the money coming in is very important. Examples of finance goals could be how much you want to make, what percentage you want to save, how much you want to invest to grow your assets, etc. I find that people do not pay enough attention to finance goals, which is a dangerous way to live because the chances of getting stranded financially then becomes very high.

Pillar 6: Firm

This speaks to whatever you find your hands doing. If you are a student, your school is your firm; if you are in paid employment, your organization is your firm. If you are a businessperson, your company is your firm. So, *what are your goals to make sure that you grow and succeed in your firm as an individual?* For example, for me as a businessperson, some of my firm goals are to grow recurrent revenue, build a strong community, publish my books, etc. These and many more are the things I need to keep my firm growing and succeeding. What are yours?

Pillar 7: Facilitate

Warren Buffett once said, "If you're in the luckiest one per cent of humanity, you owe it to the rest of humanity to think about the other 99 per cent." *Facilitate* refers to your plan to give back and add value to the wider society. For example, you can set a goal to impact one life and to give back to one person every day. It could be through the content that you share online, or phone calls made to support someone going through a rough patch. It could be a visit to the motherless babies' homes, a contribution to orphanages or other charities, or whatever you consider as being necessary to help other people succeed.

Pillar 8: Friendship

Who is a friend? The best answer I can give to this question is in the immortal words of Nobel Prize winner in Literature, Toni Morrison: "She is a friend of mind. She gathers me, man. The pieces I am, she gathers them and give them back to me in all the right order. It's good, you know, when you got a woman who is a friend of your mind."

Nobody can exist in this world alone; we all need people. We do not necessarily need too many, between five and ten really great friends that mean a lot to us and vice versa is sufficient. True friendships are great blessings that improve and enrich our lives significantly. I once read a book that talked about having your top six friends, people that you share a deep bond with, people that can carry your casket if anything happens. If you will pursue a friendship goal, finding your top six people should be it. *Do you currently have such people in your life? What can you do to nourish those relationships?* You need to have a goal to nurture those relationships and be deliberate about reaching out to them to keep the fire burning. Life can be so full of distractions to the extent that one forgets about these things, and if a person is not careful, they can drift off and become isolated. So, friendship goals are crucial to achieving a well-balanced life.

Pillar 9: Fun

Most people live life postponing the day that they will have fun and truly live! They postpone the day that they will enjoy this world. This is a truly tragic way to live. As you work hard, you must make time to have fun and do the things that you love doing and spend time with those that you love and have fun building memories with them. If you are not deliberate about creating fun goals, it is never likely to happen.

Pillar 10: Future

It is always very good to set big goals, goals that speak to the destination of your dreams, goals that go as far as five to fifteen years into the future. However, to ensure that you achieve this long-term goal, you must build all your other steps in this framework to help you. Break this big goal into shorter timelines that ensure that you remain on track and do not derail. This is important because many times, distant deadlines discourage action and kill dreams. Might I also add that the bigger the dreams the better.

Jim Rohn once said, "Become a millionaire not for the million dollars, but for what it will make of you to achieve it." For me that is very powerful. So, the bigger the goal the better, because as you journey towards this goal, you will outgrow your weaknesses and polish off all the chinks in your armor holding you down. A big goal will make sure that you go much further than you would have if you had only set a small goal.

How to use the 10-Fs Goal Setting Framework

To ensure that you succeed with this goal setting framework, you will need to keep your goals in each section down to a maximum of three, because if they are too many, you will lose focus. So, identify your Top Three Goals for each section.

After you have identified your Top Three Goals (TTG), you will need to identify and schedule the Key Actions (KA) that are required to execute these goals. And then, of course, you will need to establish your Success Measures (SM) that clearly indicate whether you have been successful.

The Only Way to Achieve Great Results

Regardless of how fantastic or highly acclaimed a goal setting methodology is, it will not work for you or anyone else if you do not devote time every day to working on it and executing your Key Actions. Execution, therefore, is the all-time secret formula to great achievements. And from personal experience, I have found that the only way to stay ahead of the enemies of execution is to *Time Block*.

Time blocking is a time management method that requires you to divide your day into blocks of time, in minutes or hours. Each block is then dedicated to accomplishing a specific task or group of tasks, and only those specific tasks. Time blocking mandates that instead of keeping an open-ended to-do list of things that you will get to as soon as you are able to, you start each day with a concrete schedule that lays out what exactly you will work on and when.

Time blocking is the only strategy that I know that successfully wards off the enemies of execution. Therefore, to achieve the extraordinary results and balanced life that you desire, you MUST daily create the time blocks that you need to execute the Key Actions for your goals ahead of time and stick to that schedule devotedly.

A final word on Goal Setting

Goal setting literally allows you to control your own destiny. So, it has always surprised me that something so life enabling is not being taught in our schools. Mountains can be moved when goals are well set and executed. Mankind has achieved great feats by goal setting. Empires have been built by goal setting. Again, I ask, why isn't goal setting rigorously taught to young children? Why is this powerful practice not being ingrained in their psyche?

I believe that it is a great injustice to not equip young people with this life transforming practice. We shall do well to work on changing that. Please commit to mastering the art and science of goal setting, and then teach it to your children, the next generation.

Key Takeaways

- The advice that what you do not know cannot hurt you is a terrible piece of advice!

- Of all the things that you do not know that can hurt you very badly, the knowledge of the critical importance of setting goals and following up on them ranks right at the top.

- Mankind has achieved great feats and empires have been built by goal setting. Not having goals and trying to navigate your life, business or career is akin to a hunter going into the forest to hunt and firing his arrow or gun indiscriminately in the hope that a deer will run into a bullet. This is probably the worst strategy anyone can adopt for living. However, most people are guilty of living their lives without setting goals.

- People who do not set goals for their lives do not appreciate the sheer power that setting and achieving goals brings into their lives. And even for those that know a thing or two about the importance of goal setting, that knowledge benefits them very little because they do not know how to set the right goals.

- The *10-Fs of Goal Setting Framework* is a comprehensive framework that will help you set goals in all the critical areas of your life, so that you can create a balanced life. Take the Wheel of Life test to examine your life as a whole. It will give you an 'helicopter' and an immediate overview of your current life balance.

- Given the power of goal setting, the greatest injustice we can do to the next generation is to fail to teach them this life transforming practice. We can work to change that by committing to master the art and science of goal setting, and then teaching it to your children—the next generation.

- Goal setting literally allows you to control your own destiny.

CHAPTER 6

MAKE FRIENDS AND GET COMFORTABLE WITH FAILURE & MISTAKES

"Failure should be our teacher, not our undertaker."
- Dennis Waitley

What if I don't succeed on this job? What if they don't buy into my idea/proposal? What if I make a fool of myself during this presentation? What if my question sounds stupid?

These and a thousand other 'what-ifs' plague every person, and yet, despite these fear-based questions, some people still act and thrive. Others allow the fear of failing at something or making a mistake put a lid on their potential.

If you wish to achieve significant success in your career or business, you must be extremely aware that two forces consistently contend for your mind. Whichever of these two forces you respond to will greatly affect your actions and ultimately determine your outcomes. The first of these forces is fear. The second is faith.

The Truth about the Fear of Failure

Everyone feels fear, but not everyone succumbs to it. Unfortunately, far too many people succumb to fear's tyranny and one of the symptoms of this submission is an excessive dread about making mistakes. The fear of failure is perfectly understandable, after all, failure sucks. I have experienced colossal failure and I have experienced phenomenal success. So, I know what both feel like. However, there is something of utmost importance that you should understand about failure. Failure is not your enemy. Fear, often cloaked as paralysis by analysis, is the real enemy.

While the Oxford dictionary defines failure as "a lack of success owing to the neglect or omission of an expected or required action" (feedback), fear is defined as "a strong and unpleasant feeling triggered by the perception of danger, pain, or harm" (feeling).

With these distinct definitions of 'fear' and 'failure', several things immediately become obvious. First, sometimes, without failing at something, there is no logical way to differentiate what works from what doesn't work. The question you need to ask yourself then becomes: *If I do not make mistakes, how then can I learn? Why is the need to not make mistakes so overpoweringly important?*

Second, since failure is simply feedback that there is an outstanding action required for success, the logical way to think about failure should be to ask yourself: *What do I need to know to succeed?*

Third, since fear is but a feeling, a negative state of mind triggered by my choice to *perceive* something as harmful or painful, I must probe this choice by asking: *Why do I choose to feel threatened by the very thing that is the key to my future success? What can I begin to do to make failure feel less threatening?*

These are some of the ways that I would like you to begin to think about your fear of failure, because if there is only one thing that I have learnt after twenty years of building a business, it is that taking well-thought-out risks while being friendly with failures and mistakes is the only way to get to the top of one's career or business. Failure and progress are interwoven, giving you two choices. Get comfortable with trying and failing or get comfortable with being average. And whichever choice is made has nothing to do with the level of an individual's intelligence.

As a matter of fact, I have a friend who happens to be one of the most intelligent people I know. This gentleman has worked very hard to cross the line of unquestioned competence. However, as at the time of writing this book, he was still struggling financially. And badly so. His biggest obstacle was his deathly fear of making a mistake and getting things wrong. He refused to venture out to take on higher roles in his career or to start his own business because of his need for certainty, which I must say was of demonic proportions. Unfortunately for my friend, his desire for 'certainty' greatly outweighed his desire to be successful.

After trying unsuccessfully to get him to venture more out of his 'safe' zone, one day, I asked him what the worst-case scenario would be if he tried something new and failed. He replied that it would set him back, and that people would begin to see him as a failure. I responded that he was already behind, and as for what others might say or think, the most tried and tested recipe for failure is the need to please people.

Whether you are a businessperson or a career professional, it is so vital to recognize that failing does not make you a failure, and failure is not a sin. People do not fail because they make mistakes; they fail because they do not extract the lessons that failure has to offer and do not launch out at success again.

If you let the fear of failure cripple your mind, your will, and your intellect, it will steal your creativity, productivity, and progress! If we could only count the number of destinies that the fear of failure has stolen, the jobs it has robbed, the bright ideas it has quenched and the joys of innovations that it has aborted in the wombs of people's lives, we would see it for what it really is, a robber. Every religion under the sun has something to say about fear. And majority of them call for resistance against this foe.

At every turn, we are surrounded by many lives that have yielded to the tyranny of fear. They are the men and women who live passively, in deep dread of failure and mistakes. Wistfully, they come to the end of their days on earth full of bitter disappointment because they did not reach for nor attain the goals that their hearts deeply yearned for. As far as I am concerned, this is the real definition of what it means to have failed. Therefore, it is prudent to learn how to tame the fear of failure, rather than letting the fear of failure harass you.

How to Tame Fear and Become Comfortable with Failure and Mistakes

The concept of failure is no longer theoretical for me. I have lived through some devastating failures in business, but I have come out stronger and better because of it. When people ask how I manage to keep it together in the face of daunting temporary defeat, my response is simply: faith. I neutralize my fears with faith.

Contrary to what some people think, faith is not a mindless or baseless way of thinking that denies reality. To have faith is to have great trust or confidence in one's ability to overcome any obstacle. It rides on the mindset that says, "I can do this, and I will do this." Faith says, "I will either find a way or make one." Faith never says die. It is a liberating force that energizes the mind and the will. When we choose to yield to faith, our minds, wills, and emotions are energized, and when this happens the full force of our intellect is activated. It takes a lot to defeat someone whose mind, will, emotions and intellect all agree over the decision to succeed. So, my first strategy to staying ahead of fear, is to <u>resist fear and always choose faith</u>.

From my experience, one of the best ways to activate faith is with words. The words you use will determine which of the two forces rises within you: fear or faith. And so, one of the first words that I redefined for myself was the word, 'failure'. When I come to tight spots that look like downright failures, I have trained my mind to think of them as merely 'bottlenecks', or 'temporary setbacks'. Next, I changed how I interpreted the meaning of the word, 'no'. I adjusted my mind to interpret 'no' as 'not yet'. This way, I deactivated the sting of rejection and programmed the word 'no' to empower me rather than debilitate me.

I encourage you to do the same. Change what failure means to you. Consider taking it as feedback and not a final position of defeat. The most successful people view failure as the halfway mark on their journey to success, and not a destination to be avoided. Reprogram your mind to think of failure as a stepping-stone to get what you really want in life.

More than anything else, memorize this equation: **Fall 7, Rise 8**. No matter the obstacles that come against you, for as long as your 'rising' outnumbers your 'falling', you will be fine.

Embracing Uncertainty

Every career or businessperson I know craves for certainty, that is, safety and security. It is a legitimate need. Indeed, psychiatrists have found that the stress of uncertainty, especially when prolonged, is among the most insidious stressors we experience as human beings. And therefore, in the face of heightened uncertainty, most people go into 'flight mode' as a means of survival.

However, herein lies the difference between those who succeed and those who don't: *The most powerful trait that successful people have is their willingness to face and handle uncertainty.* They understand that nobody can predict tomorrow, and that heightened uncertainty will always be present. And so, they do what they can to find out what it takes to succeed and then double, triple or even 10X their efforts. As a result, the world adorns them with words like 'resilient' and 'high achiever', with some successful people even going as far as building a cult-like following around themselves. This never fails to amuse me, because anybody can be successful if they just developed their 'Uncertainty Management Capability'.

There will always be large measures of uncertainties at every turn in life. So, whatever you do, you must cure yourself of the 'Certainty Disease' if you want to go far in your life and business. A good way to start to build your uncertainty management capability is by using these four guides.

First, embrace uncertainty as the 'new normal'.

Second, reject feelings of powerlessness, take ownership of your life, and maintain your sense of personal power. The only way I know to do this is to strategize and to take action!

Third, improve your learning agility. To fail fast and intelligently, you must become a learning machine. This is my strongest and favorite weapon to tackle uncertainty.

Fourth, extract from your mistakes all the wisdom you need to succeed, and then go ahead to deploy this wisdom. Never ever fail in vain.

Till date, I still have some fear of failing or making mistakes. So, how do I deal with it?

In addition to continuously developing my uncertainty capability, I run toward my fears. And to help me do this, I draw daily inspiration from one of my favorite quotes in the world attributed to Eleanor Roosevelt, First Lady of the 32nd President of the United States, Franklin Roosevelt. The quote is, "Do one thing every day that scares you."

I call it, stripping fear of its power.

What scares you? Rejection? Making mistakes? Making a fool of yourself? Speaking in public? Whatever scares you, do it every day.

Make a habit of acting on anything that worries or terrifies you. Do not just brood on it, act fast. The actions you take do not have to be big ones, you can make them very small and easy, just take action. I have found that even small actions can chase away big fears. Fear expects no resistance from you, and so when you resist it, it slinks away. Fear has a hard time coexisting with action. *When there is action, there is no fear. When there is fear, there is no action.*

If you challenge yourself in this way daily, you will be pleasantly surprised when one day, you wake up and realize that you have lost or at least drastically reduced your fear of that thing.

You gain strength, courage, and confidence by experiencing what you fear the most every day. When you do not confront them, your fears will keep you imprisoned in your comfort zone. And the danger with the comfort zone is that it is a zone of zero growth! If you remain in your comfort zone, it will eventually hurt your future.

Remember, failure is not fatal, failure is feedback, and what do people do with feedback? They learn from it. So, join the league of successful people who run toward their fears.

Be guided by faith, not fear. Take the risk to look bad. Take the chance to lose face. Put your best thoughts out there because when you do, you can only receive corrections. Be real. Be vulnerable. Be human. Just breathe. The only thing that can happen when you leave your comfort zone is that you will grow. So, give yourself a chance to grow.

Step out of your comfort zone today and start doing the things you fear the most. It will change your life dramatically!

Key Takeaways

- Two forces constantly contend for your mind. Whichever of these two forces you respond to will greatly affect your actions and ultimately determine your outcomes. One force is fear, the other is faith.

- Failure is not your enemy. Fear, cloaked as paralysis by analysis, is the real enemy. Failure and progress are interwoven, so you either get comfortable with trying and failing, or with being average.

- The fear of failure cripples your mind, your will, and your intellect, ultimately stealing your creativity, productivity, and progress!

- Change what failure means to you. Simply take it as feedback and not a final position of defeat. Reprogram your mind to think of failure as a stepping-stone to getting what you really want in life.

- Instead of fear, practice faith. The most powerful trait that successful people have is their willingness to face and handle uncertainty. They understand that nobody can predict tomorrow, and that heightened uncertainty may always be present. And so, they do what they can to find out what it takes to succeed and then double, triple or even 10X their efforts.

- To cure yourself of the need for certainty, build your uncertainty management capability by:
  i. Embracing uncertainty as the 'new normal'.
  ii. Rejecting feelings of powerlessness and taking ownership of your life.
  iii. Improving your learning agility.
  iv. Extracting the wisdom you need to succeed from your mistakes, and then going ahead to deploy this wisdom. Never ever fail in vain.
  v. "Do one thing every day that scares you". It strips fear of its power over you.

CHAPTER 7

FOLLOW THE PRINCIPLE OF NEXT

"The oak fought the wind and was broken, the willow bent when it must and survived."

- Robert Jordan

I am a very strong believer in the philosophy that the price for success is hard work, dedication to the job at hand, determination, and everything between, excluding sin and crime. And so, when I set a target or a goal for myself, I go over and beyond to make it happen because I firmly believe that with excellent preparation and hard work, everything is achievable. But this has not always been the case. There have been many times when despite my hardest works and best efforts, I have failed spectacularly because of circumstances that were beyond my control.

I recall a period in the early stages of my business when it seemed as if all I did was move from one failure to another. And as this was happening, I became aware that I was not correctly dealing with the psychological impact of each failure. The negative effect of repeated setbacks on my psyche was compounding quickly, and I finally realized that if something did not change in my mindset, it was only a matter of time before my self-confidence and self-belief took a devastating hit.

Even though I understood theoretically that failure was not meant to be taken personally, because it could have a crushing effect on a person's mental wellbeing, I did not have the psychological strategy to manage the phase of setbacks that I was experiencing. Knowing that a cycle of failures could prove to be self-perpetuating only served to compound my worries. I became desperate to find a way to ensure that I did not lose my confidence and belief because of those failures. I sought for knowledge on methods I could use to sustain my self-confidence and belief in the face of repeated disappointments and setbacks.

During my search, I stumbled upon one of the most powerful and life changing principles I have ever learnt, and I termed it, the *Principle of Next*. As simple as this principle is, it has played a mammoth role in the success I have achieved till date. I have absolutely no doubt that the principle will be of great help to everyone who is determined to succeed and willing to go the extra mile.

The *Principle of Next* basically states that *the key to sustaining self-confidence and belief in the pursuit of significant success is to recognize that no single opportunity is all-important. To be able to sustain momentum and continue to make progress even in the face of repeated and discouraging setbacks, an individual must possess the ability to say "next!" and move on quickly to the next opportunity without breaking a sweat when things don't work out.*

This principle is life transforming for the simple reason that day-to-day failure is an integral part of long-term success. Having the mental toughness to move quickly to the next opportunity when the one you have been banking on falls apart, is critical to sustaining your momentum towards success. In fact, if you take it a step further by anticipating a barrage of short-term setbacks, you will find that it has the positive effect of significantly reducing the impact of failures on your state of mind when they occur. This in turn gives you the staying power that paves the way for the birth of long-term success.

This realistic approach to business and to life fully accounts for the fact that in every situation, there is a high probability that circumstances can be beyond a person's control. From experience, most people tend to be unrealistic in their approach to pursuing their objectives. Despite knowing through personal experiences that no matter how well prepared we are, most situations in life do not work out as planned, we still remain unrealistic.

I have since concluded that the only way I can safeguard against the destruction of my inner confidence is to acknowledge the reality that, whether I like it or not, many opportunities will not deliver the expected success. In the long run, what has been the outcome of operating from this conclusion? Did it help? Brilliantly! My business experience was completely transformed within the first six months of implementing the *Principle of Next*. I am totally certain that I would not have attained the success I have so far achieved without this principle. It has enabled me to prepare for long-term success by building my immunity against the effects of short-term failures.

However, this principle works only when I have prepared adequately and worked very hard to succeed. It does not work when I approach an opportunity with laxity or when I hide behind the principle as an excuse to fail in a situation where it may have been possible to succeed had I tried harder or been more persistent. The principle works together with one of my favorite Sir Richard Branson quotes; "Opportunity is like a bus... another one is coming around soon." Whatever you do, do not allow a single missed or bungled opportunity sink you or get you stuck. You must develop the capability to put things in perspective, say 'Next' and move on.

So, if you find yourself going through the hell of back-to-back failures, keep going. Don't you dare stop. Do not make your bed there. Keep moving. Forget yesterday's mistakes. Forget yesterday's failures. Forget everything except what you are going to do NEXT and then go right ahead and do it! Yesterday is gone, today is your lucky day. Just keep moving. The gate of success awaits you at the borders of failure. Adopting the *Principle of Next* will serve you very well in your journey to achieving your highest dreams. I guarantee you.

Key Takeaways

- I strongly believe the philosophy that the price for success is hard work, dedication to the job at hand, determination, and every good thing in between. Sadly, this does not always prove to be the case. There will be times when despite one's hardest works and best efforts, failure still arises because of circumstances beyond one's control.

- When one experiences repeated failure, there is a need for a psychological coping strategy to manage this phase of setbacks being experienced. I found a powerful coping mechanism and a life changing principle, and I termed it the *Principle of Next*.

- The *Principle of Next* states that the key to sustaining self-confidence and belief in the pursuit of significant success is to recognize that no single opportunity is all-important. To sustain momentum and continue to make progress even in the face of repeated and discouraging setbacks, an individual must possess the ability to say "next!" and move on quickly to the next opportunity without breaking a sweat when things don't work out.

- This principle is life transforming because day-to-day failure is an integral part of long-term success, and so having a coping mechanism and the mental toughness to move quickly to the next opportunity when the one you have banked on falls apart, is critical to sustaining your momentum towards success.

- However, this principle works only when I have prepared adequately and worked very hard to succeed. It does not work when I approach the opportunity with laxity or when I hide behind the principle as an excuse to fail in a situation where it may have been possible to succeed had I tried harder or was more persistent.

- The Principle of Next works together with one of Sir Richard Branson quotes which says: "Opportunity is like a bus... another one is coming around soon." Whatever you do, do not allow a single missed or bungled opportunity sink you or get you stuck. You must develop the capability to put things in perspective, say 'Next' and move on.

CHAPTER 8

ADDICTION TO LEARNING & PERSONAL DEVELOPMENT: THE BEST STRATEGY FOR GETTING AND STAYING AHEAD (1)

"In times of change, learners inherit the Earth, while the learned find themselves beautifully equipped to deal with a world that no longer exists."

- Eric Hoffer

I have a confession.

I am an incurable learning addict! My addiction to learning is at level 7, meaning that I am completely and irretrievably lost to it. And I absolutely love it! I am happiest and most fulfilled when I am learning.

I start to get the blues when I have not engaged in significant learning activities in a short while, and by that, I mean 3 to 5 days maximum. Once I become aware that I am feeling low, I engage in some form of learning and almost immediately, I start to feel better. Some people love travelling; others love dancing. Some love sports, while others love partying. I love learning! I am convinced that nothing is more uplifting and life-changing than learning. Unquestionably nothing!

About 8 years ago, I attended a week-long, life-altering and perception-expanding programme at one of the leading business schools in the world. The programme was beyond good, so much so that on the last day, as soon as I stepped out of the building where the course had held, I just started running, running, and running. I promise you, I am not making this up. Till this day, I don't know why I ran, but all I can remember is that I was so happy that all I wanted to do was run. My excitement knew no limits; I just kept running until I was completely out of breath. It was one of the happiest days of my life. A day I will never forget. Yes, I am that crazy about learning.

Weird, you may think.

Well, if you have benefited as much as I have from learning and personal development, you may understand why my love affair with learning and growth is so intense. My unwavering commitment to learning and personal development has taken me places that, to be honest, were beyond my wildest dreams. I have invested millions of naira in learning. I have over 2,000 books in my library, most of them bestsellers (books that have sold more than 100,000 copies). I have been to many of the top business schools in the world in my quest for knowledge. I have personally met and learnt from some of the most knowledgeable and influential experts in the world—people like Richard Koch (best-selling author of *The 80/20 Principle*), Jim Collins (best-selling author of *Good to Great*) and my personal favorite author of all time Michael E Gerber (best-selling author *of The E-Myth Revisited*). By the way, if you have not read these and other books by these authors, shall we just say that you are missing out on your personal development big time. And that is putting it mildly. My love for learning also introduced me to my second love, teaching (I shared a lot on this in my second book, *You Must Become A Trainer*).

Incidentally, my love for learning and personal growth is also the root cause of most of my conflict with people. I struggle to relate with people who do not take complete and total ownership of their learning and personal growth. It is one of my greatest sources of frustration. There are way too many people who are not interested in their own personal growth and development and who erroneously believe that it is someone else's responsibility to develop them or push them to grow. I find this belief truly perplexing.

Fortunately, or unfortunately (depending on how you choose to see it), I enforce a personal policy of "You must develop by force" for those that I work with. If you are around me, you must abide by that principle. And it is both shocking and saddening that I have had to follow through with the consequences for not having a learning and personal development mindset with several of my former colleagues, many of whom were very talented people.

Speaking of talent, when Calvin Coolidge, the 30th President of the United States said, "nothing is more common than unsuccessful people with talent," he was right on the money! I have found that the greatest enemy of many talented people is a bloated estimation of their talents alone in driving them to succeed.

Talent Vs. Targeted Learning

It is often said that talent is performance minus effort, and herein lies the problem. As a matter of fact, the danger with too much talent is that people tend to rely solely on their talent. They adopt the false belief that they do not need to completely own their growth through continuous and never-ending learning and application.

After attaining certain heights because of their talent, unwary talented people expect to sustain excellent performance without going the extra mile to improve themselves by continuous targeted learning. This fixed growth mindset predisposes them to giving up when they encounter the roadblocks that limited knowledge always presents, and this phenomenon has been identified as the *talent trap*. Consequently, being too talented can be a stumbling block on one's way to achieving success.

How some people expect to do well in today's highly complex, volatile, and uncertain world without constantly developing themselves is completely beyond me. How they hear people like Charles Munger, Warren Buffet, Bill Gates, and a host of other globally recognized great achievers extol the virtues of lifelong learning, but still fail to realize that there must be some truth to this success strategy remains mind boggling to me. Surely, talent has its rewards, but when compared to the rewards that targeted and continuous learning brings, the difference is like night and day. Without lifelong learning, no one should expect to do very well for very long, because they can only go so far in life based on what they already know.

I consider myself very lucky to have recognized early enough that I was not talented enough not to be a committed and lifelong student. I just did not have that chance. At the beginning of my business career, when I observed certain extremely talented individuals struggling, it made me realize early that talent alone was not enough, there had to be more. In my search for what truly worked (especially for non-talented people like me), I found that working hard at learning and application was the key.

In fact, not being very talented has been a tremendous blessing in disguise for me. I am sure glad that I am not as talented as most of the talented but struggling people in business. You keep the talent, and I keep my learning and growth mindset.

Targeted Learning Trumps Talent

When you depend exclusively on talent to ascend the heights of your career or business, you leave too much to chance and you risk unpredictable results and even downright failure. The fact is that talent cannot stand on its own because it is much too frail to withstand the winds of change. Talent only gives you a head start; hard work and continuous learning is the strengthening factor that keeps you going and performing at high levels for prolonged periods. Without hard work, all the head starts in the world would not do you any good in the long run.

I have found that individuals who engage in consistent targeted learning and self-development out-perform their talent-dependent peers for these two reasons. One, being self-motivated learners means that they have mastered the art of self-leadership and self-discipline. And two, being continuous learners means that they gain the benefits of compounded knowledge.

The idea of compound knowledge rises from the fact that learning one new idea or reading one or two books does not necessarily put anyone ahead of others. It is the consistent accumulation of properly targeted knowledge that makes lifelong learning truly transformative.

In the words of Charles Munger, "You must know the big ideas in the big disciplines and use them routinely—all of them, not just a few... I went through life constantly practicing this model of disciplinary approach. I can't tell you what that's done for me. It's made life more fun. It's made me more constructive. It's made me more helpful to others. It's made me enormously rich."

Anyone can work hard at being a student as it requires zero talent, which works perfectly for the kind of person that I am. Over the years, I have studied my patterns of success and failure, and without hesitation, I would say that these two formulas account for how I function and thrive as a human.

No ownership of my learning and growth = Decline.

Full ownership of my learning and growth = Progress.

Taking Ownership of your Learning & Development

So, how can you own your learning and personal growth? What critical learning should you own and engage in to get the best results from your efforts? The answer depends on your context or situation.

For example, there have been several occasions when I read a book, and my eyes popped in wonder, and I think, "Oh my God! This is ah-mazing!" Eager to pass on my excitement, when I shared the book with the people in my network, some read a chapter or two and dropped the book, saying that they were not "feeling the book" and that maybe I had exaggerated a little about how good the book was. I have also had the reverse experience where someone recommended a book as an absolute read, and after I read the book, I thought it was average at best.

The reason for the differences in experience is simply differences of current context. It is as the popular adage says, *different strokes for different folks*. The explanation is simple. Because individuals are going through different experiences or situations in any given period, the chances are high that what one person considers game-changing learning is for another person a good read at best, and vice versa.

Your context or your current reality matters when it comes to deciding what to learn and how much benefit you would derive from it. You are more likely to get the most out of your investment in learning if the learning directly addresses your current biggest challenge or opportunity. This is where the idea of *targeted learning* comes from. Therefore, my advice to people is, *Go to school on your biggest challenges or opportunities*. That way, what you learn will not only have an immediate impact on your current situation, but the impact will also be long lasting because you would have witnessed first-hand the effects it had on your outcomes.

Be that as it may, there are some critical subject areas I have found to be relatively context-agnostic, meaning, irrespective of your context, learning these will make a huge difference in your journey of success. These types of learning also have a second and very important characteristic, they are pervasive in nature, applicable to a wider audience.

Below are some of my all-time favorite subjects. I believe that everyone should invest in learning these things irrespective of their present circumstances. The payoff on learning them is immense. This list of learning intervention has grown over the years, and it is still growing. I call this, the *BO Learning Inventory*, and I am delighted to share them with you in the hope that they will benefit you as much as they have benefited me over the years.

The BO Learning Inventory
Learn:

1. About yourself
2. How to learn
3. How to get along with others
4. How to succeed
5. About the importance of reality
6. How to manage time wisely
7. How to manage money
8. How to manage emotions
9. The discipline of getting things done
10. How to lead without authority
11. How to teach
12. How to manage people
13. How to run a business
14. How to think
15. How to speak in public/present
16. How to write effectively
17. How to have fun/recreate
18. How to negotiate
19. How to sell effectively
20. About marketing
21. To network & build relationships
22. How to hire right
23. How to change and adapt
24. How to focus/concentrate
25. How to make effective decisions
26. How to influence & persuade people
27. How to ask good questions
28. How to follow through
29. How to gain insights
30. How to get what you want
31. How to conduct research
32. How to plan & organize
33. How to serve others
34. How to meditate
35. How not to fail
36. How to be indispensable
37. How to look good and classy
38. How to prepare
39. How to get unstuck
40. How to develop a bias for action
41. How to tell inspiring stories
42. How to be excellent/exceptional
43. How to create and use checklists
44. How to build self-confidence
45. How to keep healthy and fit
46. How to simplify
47. How to leverage
48. To identify & grow your strengths
49. How to drive performance
50. How to say NO
51. To create multiple streams of income
52. How to be self-disciplined
53. How to tell jokes
54. To be digitally savvy
55. How to cope with adversity
56. To keep journals and records
57. To seek and get help
58. How to set goals
59. How to write a book
60. How to become an effective consultant

If you desire success, the starting point is to take full and total ownership of your learning and personal growth. The *BO Learning Inventory* is a very good place to start, and I can assure you that it will transform your life as it has mine. Trust me.

Key Takeaways

Being too talented can be a stumbling block on one's way to achieving success. The danger with too much talent is that people tend to rely only on their talent. They adopt the false belief that they do not need to take complete ownership of their growth through continuous and unending learning and application.

After attaining certain heights because of their talent, unwary talented people expect to sustain excellent performance without going the extra mile to improve themselves by continuous targeted learning. This fixed growth mindset predisposes them to giving up when they encounter the challenges that limited knowledge always brings, and this phenomenon has been identified as the *talent trap*.

While talent only gives you a head start, hard work and continuous learning is the strengthening factor that keeps you going and performing at high levels for prolonged periods. Without hard work all the head starts in the world will not do you any good in the long run.

Talent certainly has its rewards, but when compared to the rewards that targeted continuous learning bring, the difference is like night and day. Without lifelong learning, no one should expect to do very well for very long, because they can only go so far in life based on what they already know.

Individuals who engage in consistent targeted learning and self-development out-perform their talent dependent peers because as self-motivated learners, they have mastered the art of self-leadership and self-discipline. And as continuous learners, they gain the benefits of compounded knowledge.

Anyone can work hard at being a student, it requires zero talent. My formulas for success are:

No ownership of my learning and growth = Decline.

Full ownership of my learning and growth = Progress.

Your context or your current reality matters when it comes to choosing what to learn and how much benefit you would derive from it. You are more likely to get the most out of your investment in learning if it directly addresses your current biggest challenge or opportunity.

Go to school on your biggest challenges or opportunities. That way, what you learn will not only have an immediate impact on your current situation, but the impact will also be long lasting because you would have witnessed the effects it had on your outcomes.

CHAPTER 9

ADDICTION TO LEARNING & PERSONAL DEVELOPMENT: THE BEST STRATEGY FOR GETTING AND STAYING AHEAD (2)

> *"There is no better teacher than history in determining the future … There are answers worth billions of dollars in a $30 history book."*
>
> **- Charles Munger**

Over a decade ago, in my search for the wisdom that guaranteed business and life success, I stumbled upon one of the most powerful lessons I have learned till date. This lesson is very dear to me for two reasons. First, it has been the foundation for everything that I have done since encountering it. Second, it is the foundation for everything I will ever do today and in my future.

It all began the day I decided to analyze what I refer to as my *ROL, Return on Learning.* After spending much time analyzing the returns on my knowledge investment, I quickly realized that some of my investments in learning had added so much value to me but not so much from others. Being the unrepentant capitalist that I am, I was keen to find out how to optimize my learning and development related activities and investment.

I wanted to know what worked, what didn't, and why. Where were the gaps? What were the differences between learning that produced superior returns and learning that just provided information? I wanted to know how I could replicate my successful learning activities and minimize the unsuccessful ones. Essentially, I was looking for a formula that worked to make a learner like me succeed predictably. Around the same time, a senior friend and mentor introduced me to the world of biographies and autobiographies. From that point on, everything changed. I mean, everything!

For a pragmatic learner who loves to learn from successful people on what truly worked, everything else paled into insignificance when compared to learning from biographies and autobiographies. And as I went on to discover, the older the biographies and autobiographies, the better. Some of the old ones are so difficult to read and comprehend that if you are not a disciplined reader and learner, they can easily become very potent sleeping pills. This was perfect for me because it meant that few people would make the effort to read them, meaning less competition (did I mention that I am by nature very competitive?).

My coach recommended that I start by reading a couple of biographies and autobiographies. One of the recommended ones that made a world of difference to me was the *Autobiography of Benjamin Franklin*. It was within the pages of Benjamin Franklin's autobiography that I found one of the most profound secrets to becoming a successful learner.

Benjamin Franklin was a printer, writer and publisher based in Philadelphia in the 17th Century. At some point, he was struggling in business and badly in debt. Frustrated with his situation, he desperately wanted to turn it around. He thought to himself that if only he could find the right method and rhythm for owning his personal growth and development and one that was practical and easy to follow consistently, he could learn and acquire the essential principles of success. He decided to tackle this challenge head-on. After struggling for a while, he developed a simple but very effective method for becoming a lifelong learner. This method is so practical that I have been modifying and using it for well over a decade with exceptional and outsized results.

Below is an explanation of how he took ownership of his learning and went on to become a phenomenally successful statesman.

Benjamin Franklin chose 13 subjects based on his perception of what was required for success. He dedicated a week to thoroughly studying and mastering each of the subjects.

Choosing 13 subjects over 13 weeks enabled him to repeat the process 4 times in a year ($13 \times 4 = 52$ weeks a year), thus ensuring he attained his desired level of mastery.

Just imagine this with me. Here was one of the greatest geniuses that ever lived. And what was the secret to his success? He became a lifelong student and took complete responsibility for his personal development and growth.

He went on to write, "I hope, therefore, that some of my descendants may follow the example and reap the benefits."

You bet Mr. Franklin! Even though I am not one of your descendants. You bet!

Below is Benjamin Franklin's list of 13 subjects as it appeared in his autobiography:

1. **Temperance:** Not to dullness; do not drink to elevation.

2. **Silence:** Only speak what may benefit others or yourself; avoid trifling conversation.

3. **Order:** Let all your things have their places; let each part of your business have its time.

4. **Resolution:** Resolve to perform what you should; perform without what you resolve.

5. **Frugality**: Make no expense but to do good to others or yourself, that is, waste nothing.

6. **Industry:** Lose no time, be always employed in something useful; cut off all unnecessary action.

7. **Sincerity:** Refuse hurtful deceit; think and speak innocently and justly.

8. **Justice:** Do wrong to none by injuries or omitting the benefits that are your duty to provide.

9. **Moderation:** Avoid extremes, forbear resenting injuries so much as you think they deserve.

10. **Cleanliness:** Disallow all uncleanliness in your body, clothes, or habitation.

11. **Tranquility:** Do not be disturbed at trifles or at accidents common or avoidable.

12. **Chastity:** Avoid venery, but for health or offspring, never to dullness, weakness, or the injury of your own or another's peace or reputation.

13. **Humility:** Imitate Jesus and Socrates.

(Note: On that thirteenth one, I will rather stick with Jesus. Socrates is too much of a stretch for me!)

Benjamin Franklin's list and methodology had such a profound impact on my life. I was so taken by its simplicity and practicality that I immediately created my own list of 13 subjects and started my personal 13 weeks' cycle of learning and personal growth journey. From the moment I began until this day, it has indeed been an experience that keeps broadening my perspective.

Since creating my own version of Benjamin Franklin's Learning List, over the years, I have changed items on the list to reflect my ongoing realities, contexts, and the urgent knowledge gaps that I needed to close. It has been a truly rewarding experience.

My very first 13 subjects are listed below.

1. Productivity and Time Optimization

2. Emotional Intelligence

3. Training and Facilitation

4. Sales and Marketing

5. Running a Business

6. HR and Consulting

7. Strategic Thinking, Planning and Execution

8. Talent Management

9. Leadership

10. Personal Development

11. Finance

12. Relationship Management

13. Writing

My ongoing pattern has been to complete each 13-week cycle and start all over again while ensuring that I keep my list for at least one year. Some of the items on my list have been there for many years.

Sometimes, I fall off my learning rhythm for a long spell of time, and I suffer the consequences in decline and struggle. But once I find my way back, it is usually only a matter of time before I start making progress again. The predictable nature of the outcomes of this process is truly remarkable.

What about you? Do you have a structure around your personal learning and growth? Do you have a rhythm that ensures that you learn consistently and continue to grow from the standpoint of competency? Or is your approach to learning and growth haphazard and ill-structured?

Trust me, you will benefit greatly from some sort of structure. You are more than welcome to copy and contextualize Benjamin Franklin's model or mine.

You will be glad you did.

Key Takeaways

- There is significant wisdom to be found in biographies and autobiographies. The older the biographies and autobiographies, the better.

- Benjamin Franklin's secret to success was his habit of lifelong learning. He completely took ownership of his personal development and growth.

- Create a structure around your personal learning and growth. Have a rhythm that ensures that you learn consistently and continue to grow in terms of competencies. Do not approach your learning and growth haphazardly.

- Create your personal reading plan. You are more than welcome to copy and contextualize Benjamin Franklin's model.

CHAPTER 10

WHY ARE YOU NOT DOING WELL? HOW ASKING THE RIGHT QUESTIONS CAN TRANSFORM YOUR CAREER OR BUSINESS

"The important and difficult job is never to find the right answers. It is to find the right question."

- Peter Drucker

It became obvious that there was something deeply wrong with Bade, when for the umpteenth time in less than an hour he had answered all the questions I directed at him with a blank and absent-minded stare.

I suspected that things were not going well with his job because he had mentioned it once or twice in our previous conversations. But when he had not given any more details on the matter, despite my gentle nudging, I pulled back from probing further and assured him that if he ever needed to talk, I was available.

But since that conversation, Bade never mentioned his job again. However, as he sat in front of me, I did not need a soothsayer to tell me that trouble was brewing. I could tell by his premature aging looks, his blank stare, and unsettling silence, even when he was amidst old friends, that he was fast approaching his breaking point.

"Bade, why are you not doing well?" I asked.

Bade froze, blinked several times in surprise, and said, "Excuse me, what did you say?"

I repeated my question, this time more slowly, with deeper emphasis on his name and the 'why' part of the question.

"BADE, WHY are you not doing well? Have you asked yourself that question?"

There was a long pause followed by a deep sigh, after which Bade broke his silence and the conversation that marked the turnaround of his shipwrecked career began in earnest.

This exchange between my long-time friend and me took place some years ago. That single question forced him to confront his brutal realities, which in turn started him on a journey of renewal and transformation. Thankfully, after several coaching sessions and some major work with a mentor, Bade pulled through and went on to enjoy resounding success in his career.

Perhaps he would have found his feet eventually, or perhaps not, we would never know. But one thing we do know is that prior to my thought-provoking question to him, Bade had been horribly stuck, finding it difficult to make progress in his career. That question put him on a new path by forcing him to reflect deeply on the root cause of what was preventing him from making the progress he wanted.

The Nature of Questions

Good questions are powerful because they jumpstart people's thinking. The right question will always serve as a source of fresh ideas that enables people to innovate, solve problems, and move ahead in their careers and in their lives.

Questions that initiate new ideas force us to think deeply, usually in a direction that we had never thought before. When this happens, a new 'file' is opened in our brains, and like Ralph Waldo Emerson rightly said, "The mind, once stretched by a new idea, never returns to its original dimensions."

Two of the most powerful gifts that the consulting and coaching professions have bequeathed to me are:

1. A profound appreciation for the power of good questions, and the understanding that knowing the right questions to ask is far greater than having quick answers.
2. The ability to ask the right questions.

The most creative and successful people tend to be expert questioners. They have mastered the art of inquiry, asking questions no one else asks and therefore, discovering powerful answers. And this inquisitive nature accelerates their careers and businesses because by being able to identify and ask questions that expand their perception, they can identify new opportunities and fresh possibilities years ahead of their competitors. This in turn places them on top of the 'food chain'.

One of the chief drivers of questioning is an awareness of what we do not know. Good questioners tend to be aware of their ignorance and are quite comfortable with it. However, herein lies the biggest challenge; most people suffer from a syndrome popularly known as *the Dunning Kruger Effect* (a type of cognitive bias in which people believe that they are smarter and more capable than they really are).

Unfortunately for those with this syndrome, because questions open the doors to possibilities, not asking questions would mean that these doors remain shut in their faces, invariably putting a peg on their growth. I consider this too high a price to pay. And so, I proudly embrace my ignorance and the vulnerability that comes from saying, "I don't know," because when I own that, the miracle of insight starts to play out.

I choose to be quite comfortable with my ignorance because it forces me to ask hard questions.

Questions like:

- What am I not seeing? What should I be seeing?
- What is it that I do not know that has the potential to keep me stuck? And what must I know to elevate my life?
- How can I become really good at what I do?
- What is one thing that is difficult to do, but if I do well, can have a game-changing impact on my life?

If you will thrive in your career or business, you cannot afford to be afraid to ask questions. Someone once told me that she was afraid to ask questions because she was worried that she would ask stupid questions. My response to her was, "there are no stupid questions." There are only gaps in knowledge that must be filled to enable the mind to generate good solutions.

Worrying more about what others think of our intelligence than what we think about improving our own thinking is a major pitfall and hindrance to living a productive life. To hide one's ignorance is to risk failure in the long term. You simply must shed that mask.

I deeply respect the things that I do not know. And I believe that this respect has helped me to achieve more success than many of my other attributes, as it *forces me to dig deep and find out what I need to know and do to succeed.*

Other critical questions for your consideration are as follows:

- How is my field/industry/organization changing?
- What trends are having the most impact on my field, and how is that likely to play out over the next few years?
- Which of my existing skills are most useful and adaptable in this new environment, and what new skills do I need to add?
- Should I diversify more, or should I focus on specializing in one area?
- Should I be thinking more in terms of finding a job or creating one?

As the world becomes more complex, questions are becoming more valuable than answers. If you want to succeed in your career or business, you need to get comfortable with your ignorance and start asking yourself tough questions and taking the time to answer them intentionally.

The right questions are the keys to unlocking the shackles of and breaking free from our self-imposed limitations. For instance, many centuries ago, before the invention of vaccines, the life expectancy of humans was very low. Life was hard, short, and painful. If men had never asked the question, "How can we tame or even eliminate dangerous diseases?" the idea of vaccination would never have been conceived. But we are so grateful that they asked that question and ran with it until the answer came.

Questions do not hinder us; they give us clarity. And clarity is key if you want to be the best in your career or business. If you ask a good question long and hard enough, the answer will come, it always does. For it is written in the fabric of nature that "they that seek will always find". It is a law of the Universe.

So, if your desire is to build a great business or career that you can be proud of, and if you believe that tomorrow will come, then there is no better way to set the ball rolling than by asking yourself this question:

What can I begin to do today to change the trajectory of my life, deeply impact my career and create the future of my dreams?

Key Takeaways

- Good questions are powerful because they jumpstart people's thinking. The right question will always serve as a source of fresh ideas that enables people to innovate, solve problems, and move ahead in their careers and lives.

- The most creative and successful people tend to be expert questioners.

- Most people suffer from a syndrome popularly known as the *Dunning Kruger Effect* (a type of cognitive bias in which people believe that they are smarter and more capable than they really are.)

- Worrying more about what others think of our intelligence than what we do about improving our own thinking is a major pitfall to living a productive life.

- To hide one's ignorance is to risk failure in the long term.

- Questions do not hinder us; they give us clarity.

CHAPTER 11

SIMPLIFY OR SUFFER

"Nature is pleased with simplicity. And nature is no dummy."

- Isaac Newton

As a business consultant, I have spent over two decades working with and studying organizations that are all over the map in terms of their sizes, industries, and business models. Throughout this time, I have seen very small businesses succeed. I have seen mid-sized companies succeed and thrive. I have seen very large organizations succeed and scale, but I have never, ever seen a complex business succeed. No, not even one!

As far as business is concerned, successful entrepreneurs will tell you this: *Small is good. Medium size is good. Big is good. Complex is never good!*

Nothing wears out the human mind faster than unnecessary complexities, whether it is a complex idea, a complex organizational infrastructure, complex technology, or anything complex at all. People struggle with complex things.

To show you what I mean, let's run a little test. Please read the two paragraphs labelled Paragraph 1 and Paragraph 2 below, and thoughtfully consider the implications of complexity. By the way, the two paragraphs express the same idea.

But before you read them, here is a short background to both.

In 1942, during World War II, President Franklin Delano Roosevelt, issued an Executive Black Out Order to Americans, and asked his assistant to write a memo instructing federal workers on what to do during an air raid. Paragraph 1 is what the assistant wrote.

Paragraph 1:

"Such preparations shall be made as will completely obscure all Federal and non-Federal buildings occupied by the Federal Government during an air raid for any period of time from visibility by reason of internal or external illumination. Such obscuration may be obtained either by black-out construction or by termination of the illumination."

It is said that Roosevelt called for the rewriting of the memo and dictated the following to the writer:

Paragraph 2:

"Tell them, that in buildings where they have to keep the work going, to put something over the windows; and, in buildings where they can let the work stop for a while, turn out the lights."

Thank you for reading the sentences. Now, let's take the test. Kindly answer the following questions:

    i.   How well did you enjoy reading sentence one?

    ii.   How easy was it for you to comprehend it?

    iii.   How many times did you read the sentence to get the message?

    iv.   How did it make you feel?

If it took a lot of willpower for you to finish reading the first sentence, congratulations! You are a normal and well-adjusted human being. Normal people struggle with the kind of complexity that was well communicated in it. When you allow yourself to get bitten by the complexity bug, the effect on you and those around you is exhausting at best, and productivity killing at worst.

Now consider the second paragraph.

    i.   How fast did you read this sentence?

    ii.   Was it easy for you to understand the message?

    iii.   Did the simplicity of the message save you time?

I am confident that your answers to these three questions are all positive.

This is what happens to you and your business when you simplify. People make less mistakes, they are less exhausted and more productive.

Simple always wins. Complex causes big problems.

Looking back on my entrepreneurial journey, I am amazed by how far out of my way I went to complicate my business life. It is honestly perplexing! What I did back then seems incomprehensible to me now. It is almost as if I was infected with the complexity virus! My irrational behavior cannot be explained another way.

All my waking hours back then were tied up in seeking ways to make things as complicated as possible. I used to make fun of myself with this statement, "If there was a way to turn something simple into a complex situation, you could count on me to not disappoint you".

The time, money, and energy I invested in complicating my business dealings represent some of my greatest regrets in business and are partly responsible for some of the grave failures I experienced along the way.

As a result of complicating my business, I never had the time, space, and resources to do the one thing that really created success: *Focusing maniacally on what mattered most and tapping into my creative ability.*

Today, with maturity and the benefits of hindsight, I am redeemed. And so, when I see people very much like my old self every day in business running around like people possessed with other-worldly powers, adding more and more complexity to their businesses and personal lives, I do my best to help them see the folly of their ways to give them the chance to adjust sooner.

Some try to impress me by showing off how intelligent they are in complicating their business. I just laugh and shake my head. Rather than being impressed, I feel very sorry for them.

Business already has inbuilt complexities, especially as it grows. It certainly does not need the owner to build in additional layers of complexity. As a matter of fact, I will argue that the biggest responsibility of a business owner is to stay alert and constantly monitor, identify, reduce, or eliminate complexity from their business. This is so important.

Write this down and take it to heart: **SIMPLIFY or SUFFER.** This is the motto I have now adopted in my business life. It might save you a lot of unnecessary headaches.

You must learn to simplify your business or suffer the consequences. A complex business will almost or eventually kill the owner. Take it from me; I know this first-hand.

So, whatever you do, keep it simple!

I once read an article on what Jeff Bezos said about Amazon. "What we do at

Amazon will never change. How we do it might change, but what we do will never change. As long as we don't forget that we will be fine. The moment we forget that our fate is sealed."

Here are some of the top reasons why I believe people complicate their business (and life).

1. *Too much intelligence.* Sometimes, the so-called smart people end up introducing complexities into what they do, just to show how smart they are. In my opinion, this is dumb, and I have been guilty of this in the past. Simplicity, not complexity, is the proof of intelligence.

2. *The erroneous belief that complexity equals uniqueness or differentiation.* Some people believe that if something is too simple, then it is probably not good enough. This is wrong because it takes more effort to simplify.

3. *Boredom.* Sometimes, some people become bored after doing something repeatedly, and in the name of innovation or creativity, they muddle it up, introduce complexity and then create crisis. They do this even when what they were doing still works very well.

4. *Inability to say No.* I have discovered that the worst kinds of complexities are the ones others introduce into your life. Hence, your inability to say no is the greatest problem you need to overcome to reduce the level of complexity in your life or business.

Complexity creates more options for failure, and complicating your business is guaranteed to distract you and make you forget what winning is primarily about, which will always leave you struggling.

Thankfully, after suffering so much from complexities, I came to the point where I could not take it anymore. It finally dawned on me that I was on a suicide mission, and I urgently needed to rethink my life and business approach completely. So, I set about eliminating complexities from my life.

In the process, I discovered that I was my own worst enemy. I realized that to get rid of complexities from my personal life and business, I needed to do these five things:

1. Identify my true goals.

2. Discover what actually works.

3. Ignore distractions.

4. Create routines.

5. Show up consistently.

These same actions will probably prove to be true for you too. The only way to save yourself from burnout and keep your business from becoming a train wreck, is to do your best to rid yourself of all unnecessary baggage and keep things as simple as possible.

Recently, a friend reached out to me asking if I wanted to participate in an activity. At the beginning, the request was straightforward and what I was asked to do was simple enough, so I indicated my interest. We agreed to speak a few days later to work out the details. When we eventually spoke, lo and behold, my dear friend had introduced a new level of complication that could only be matched by my old complicator self, all in the name of being innovative and doing something unique. With my complexity detector batteries fully charged, I was on red alert, recognizing it for what it was. Immediately and sadly, I had to decline to participate. Complexity has caused too much suffering for me, and the last thing I will ever do is to joke around with it. I just will not do it.

In the same way, I would like to encourage you to be on the alert. Learn how to detect and avoid complexity. It does not serve your ultimate purpose in life or in business. It only makes things harder than they need to be.

Complicating your business leads to a form of self-imprisonment. You will be trapped by the complexity you introduced into your business eventually. I guarantee it. So, whatever you do, avoid complexity at all costs. Keep things simple. Remember this, ***to soar, you need to travel light. To travel light, you must simplify!***

The war against complexity is an age-long one. *Occam's Razor* is a principle attributed to the 14th century logician William of Ockham. Also known as the Law of Parsimony, the principle states, "Entities should not be multiplied unnecessarily." We will all do well to abide by this advice.

So go on, simplify your life and soar!

Key Takeaways

- As far as business is concerned, successful entrepreneurs will tell you this: "Small is good. Medium size is good. Big is good. Complex is never good!" A complex business will almost or eventually kill the owner. I know this first-hand.

- Nothing wears out the human mind faster than unnecessary complexities. People struggle with complex things. Simple always wins. Complex causes big problems.

- The time, money, and energy I invested in complicating my business dealings represent some of my greatest regrets in business and are partly responsible for some of the major failures I experienced along the way.

- If you complicate your business or your life, you will never have the time, space, and resources to do the one thing that really creates success. Business already has inbuilt complexities, especially as it grows. It does not need its owner to add unnecessary layers of complexity.

- An important responsibility of a business owner is to stay alert and constantly monitor, identify, reduce, or eliminate complexities from their business.

- People complicate their business (and life) because of too much intelligence, the erroneous belief that complexity equals uniqueness or differentiation, boredom, and an inability to say 'No'.

- To get rid of complexities from your personal life and business, identify your true goals; discover what actually works; ignore distractions; create routines, and show up consistently.

- Remember this: to soar, you need to travel light. And to travel light, you must simplify!

CHAPTER 12

ARE YOUR HABITS THE CHINKS IN YOUR ARMOR?

"You do not rise to the level of your goals. You fall to the level of your systems."

- James Clear

I recently read an interesting article about *Nike*'s newest runner shoes, the *Nike Vaporfly*. It is said that the shoes literally spring runners forward and help elite runners shave precious seconds off their times. One expert said that the runner runs the race, but the shoes enable him or her to run it faster for the same effort or ability. Another kinesiology researcher went as far as predicting that if two athletes of equal ability ran on any race day, the one with the *Nike* shoes would beat the one without those shoes. The secret of *Nike Vapourfly* is said to be in the sole of the shoe, which is designed to help runners get the most forward push for each stride and helps runners run faster for the same energy spent. Naturally, some critics have called the *Vaporfly* technological doping, arguing that the shoes gave athletes an unfair advantage over competitors who were not equipped with the same technology. However, if you ask me, I will say that if the shoes are openly available to everyone willing to make the investment, it is a level playing field. Life is hard enough to go through without advantages. And so, if a support system is without sin or crime, it is acceptable to me if it helps me to beat the odds.

Obviously, this is not a lesson about *Nike* shoes. It is a lesson about the greatest and most unfair advantage a person can have in the race of business and life, that is, a lesson on the power of habits.

In all my years of participating in the marathons of life and of business, I have always researched, observed, and studied the newest findings, proven formulas, and systems on how to succeed and always stay ahead of my peers. Over the years, different success ideas, philosophies, technologies, and methodologies have come and gone. Through them all, and with no exception, I have repeatedly found that no matter how fantastic a method was, no matter how advantageous a technology or formula was, only one thing truly guaranteed success, and that is the system of habits that a person has built and operates his life with. Without equivocation, I think that just as the *Vaporfly* was said to give an unfair advantage to runners, so is a system of good and enabling habits an unfair advantage for anyone who hopes to beat the odds in life and in business.

Our daily habits are nothing more than those automatic and repeated behaviors that fill up our entire lives. Whether they are repeated ways of thinking or acting or feeling, they tie us down or they set us free. Be they are our sleeping, eating, relationship building, personal development habits, study, or work habits, they either make or break us; they either build us up or tear us apart.

Steven Pressfield, renown writer of one of the best books ever written about how to breakthrough creative barriers, noted brilliantly that, "The difference between an amateur and a professional is in their habits. An amateur has amateur habits. A professional has professional habits. We can never free ourselves from habit. But we can replace bad habits with good ones."

Habits are Stronger than Reasoning

I have soberly found habits to be stronger than reason. When you repeat the same thought or action long enough, it develops into a habit which, repeated frequently enough, eventually becomes an automatic reflex response that withstands the strongest reason. If you are truly committed to winning in life and in business, the best thing that you can therefore do for yourself is to screen your habits aggressively and continuously. Brutally evaluate yourself with the following questions:

- *Are my habits working for me or against me?*

- *Do my habits hold me back, or like* Nike Vaporfly, *do they propel me forward and cause me to gain grounds, save energy and thrive through life's 'wear and tear'?*

- *Do my habits make my life easier, or do they make my life harder?*

- *Do my habits make me richer or poorer?*

- *Do my habits make me healthier or progressively sicker?*

- *Are my habits leading me to an early grave or are they extending my life?*

Are your habits a gift or a curse?

Author and executive speechwriter Matthew Cossolotto once gave an honest account of his failure to reach his potential. He described the power and the undercurrent of ingrained behavior and thought patterns that made him a 'victim.' In his clear articulation of the unstoppable force of habits—negative habits in this case—Cossolotto recalls the day he learned that an original idea for a new TV channel that he and a business partner had toyed with and then squandered had been launched by someone else. "I had sabotaged my own success … I procrastinated; I was indecisive; I allowed myself to be side-tracked; I undermined myself with doubts about my qualifications and credentials; I failed to follow through at critical times."

He eventually began to see that those behaviors had defined his response to many aspects of his life, not just to business ideas or innovations. Habits, positive or negative, can be your default setting in life and you can put them to work instinctively, for good or bad, almost without realizing it.

Scientists have said that habits emerge because the brain is constantly looking for ways to save effort. I believe that habit as a concept is a gift, and its ultimate purpose is to help us solve the problems of life with as little energy and effort as possible. However, in the end, our habits are what we make of them. They either become our source of success or undoing, our gift or our curse.

The Oracle of Omaha is quoted to have incisively said, "The chains of habit are too light to be felt until they are too heavy to be broken." I could not agree more. Habits must not be left to themselves to run wild and free. They must be checked. Our unchecked sleeping patterns culminate into sleeping habits. Our unregulated eating patterns eventually become our eating habits. Our health care patterns become our health care habits, and the same goes for our working, thinking and other patterns in our lives.

Think about this for a minute. *When you wake up in the morning, what is the first thing that you do? What is your first thought or pattern of thoughts? What are your first actions? What are your first feelings?* Left to its own devices, the brain will try to make almost any routine into a habit, because habits allow our minds to ramp down more often. Our behavioral patterns must therefore be observed and adjusted from time to time to keep them working for us, and not against us.

Over the years, I have often found that when my daily routines are allowed to go unchecked for efficiency for long periods, many times, I find myself ensnared in unproductive and derailing habits that often require a bitter struggle to break. Specifically, negative habits of thought have been my worst enemies. And so, to keep myself from being ensnared altogether, I have since learnt to catch myself before I fall. I do it by 'sanitizing' my thoughts and behaviors by answering these powerful questions regularly.

- *Lately, how have I been habitually thinking, behaving, and living?*

- *Do these thinking and behavioral patterns make time my ally or an enemy?*

- *What is the quality of my small but routine behavioral patterns? If these behaviors were to be seeds and I kept planting them every day, what kind of fruits would I harvest a year from now, ten years from now? Would they be valuable plants that bring life? Or would they be weeds, thistles or thorns that amount to a wasted life?*

Creating a few powerful habits to alter your outcomes

Programming certain habits to create a big impact in my life is the most important thing I have learned in my adult life. I have learnt that there is nothing I cannot do if I get the corresponding habits right. I have also learnt first-hand that a small but directed amount of my efforts produces a disproportionately large amount of my results.

This is well-known as the *Pareto principle*, or the 80:20 principle. Simply put, the 80:20 rule states that the relationship between input and output is rarely, if ever, balanced. Apply this, and you will find out that approximately 20 percent of your efforts produce 80 percent of results. What you need is the ability to recognize and focus more on that 20 percent, which is the key to making the most effective use of your time.

For instance, Susanna Wesley is remembered today as the mother of brothers, John and Charles Wesley, key leaders of the Christian church in eighteenth-century England. Biographies of Susanna offer a revealing insight into the fierce devotion to the Christian faith and motherhood that characterized her life. As the mother of nineteen children, only ten of whom survived beyond infancy, Susanna had a life filled with great demands and since there was no privacy or peace to be found in the house, her habit was to pull her apron over her head to pray for a few moments, shutting out the busyness of life. This seemingly insignificant habit of carving out a tiny piece of what we today would call 'personal space,' no doubt had a much more powerful result. It enabled her to renew her strength for the tasks ahead of her while creating a pattern of disciplined focus, which were not only meaningful for her, but became an influential model for her children.

Personally, a vital part of my 20 percent of non-negotiable daily habits includes rising by 5 am and walking 10,000 steps per day. These habits are key to the structure of my day and the stability of my health, as they set the tone for my day and enable me to live the day productively. *How can you find your 20 percent? What activities produce the best outcomes for you?* Once you identify them, focus on them. Spending more time on the things that have the best chance of making the biggest difference will go a long way in making you more successful with less effort. In other words, find your non-negotiables. By focusing on these non-negotiables— the 20 percent of your activities, you are invariably obeying the 80:20 principle, thereby creating 80 percent of your results.

Habits that lead to success need practice and repetition

As human beings, we all have the tendency to default into doing the same things we did yesterday, the day before, and every day of the last month, last year and even last decade. And habits, good or bad, make us who we are. The key is to ensure we practice good habits daily till they become a part of us so that we can do them subconsciously. This is one major way to guarantee success.

Many times, people fail in life no matter how hard they work largely because of their habits of mediocrity which they have built through repetition over time. Living one successful day at a time by practicing your 20 percent non-negotiable habits guarantees that you are forming habits of success daily.

And while you are at it, it is also helpful to realize that there are some things in life that absolutely cannot be hurried. Some achievements grow rather slowly, and all that you can do is plant one habit a day at a time, year after year before you can begin to see the first harvests. There is usually no way and no shortcut to bypass this kind of life investment. It takes an accumulation of 'one habit at a time' over a long time to win. All you can do is simply grow to love or at least accept the slow process of making orderly living your habit. Love the thought that you are doing the right thing in unfolding your best destiny. Because in the end, you will only be able to reach your full potential by *breaking the habits* that no longer serve you.

Begin today to act in ways and form habits that make time an ally instead of an enemy. Whatever you do, be completely sure that your habits do not become a source of vulnerability—a chink in your armor—that causes you to fail in life or in business.

Key Takeaways

- I have since learnt that there is only one thing that truly guarantees success—the system of habits that a person builds and operates his life with.

- Habit is stronger than reason. If you are truly committed to winning in life and business, the best thing that you can do for yourself is to screen your habits aggressively and continuously.

- Often, a small, directed amount of your efforts produces a disproportionately large amount of your results. This is well-known as the 80:20 (Pareto) principle. Therefore, learning how to form habits that create big impacts in your life is an important thing you can do. There is nothing you cannot do if you get the right habits.

- People fail in life no matter how hard they work largely because of inbuilt habits of mediocrity repeated overtime. Living one successful day at a time by practicing your 20 percent non-negotiable habits guarantees that you are forming habits of success daily.

- Whatever you do, be completely sure that your habits do not become a source of vulnerability—a chink in your armor that can cause you to fail in life and in business.

CHAPTER 13

STRATEGY AND REALITY

"Good strategy grows out of an independent and careful assessment of the situation... Bad strategy follows the crowd."
- Richard P. Rumelt

In the world of business, there are a handful of small lies, big lies, and myths around the concept of strategy. Of these three, the myths about strategy are the worst. While savvy executives can easily drill to the bottom of small lies and big lies, myths are harder to detect because they are half-truths that have been peddled around for a long time and sometimes by some very respected sources. One of the biggest myths about the concept of strategy is that it is complex or complicated.

On the contrary, strategy as a concept is very simple. After years of working with companies to straighten up their business processes and facilitate their strategy sessions, I have found that companies that repeatedly get their strategy right, and win as a result, are companies that understand and accept that another word for strategy is simply, 'solution'. Despite the avalanche of opinions on how to build an effective strategy, these companies understand that the core of any good strategy is always the same. *Discover the critical, real life factors in a situation and design a way of coordinating and focusing actions to deal with those factors.* These organizations understand that they can only effectively articulate a powerful winning strategy when they accurately answer these four distinct questions.

1. Where are we? Call it Point A.
2. Where do we want to go? Call that Point B.
3. How do we get there?
4. What obstacles must we overcome to close the gap between Point A and Point B?

They understand that when they have accurately and clearly answered these questions, their strategy would emerge all by itself. Strategy, therefore, is the 'solution' they arrive at to close the identified gap between Point A and Point B.

If strategy is this straightforward, then what is the problem? Why can't many businesses or even individuals just articulate their Point A, Point B, and their gaps, and then develop a solution (strategy) to eliminate the obstacles, close the gaps and succeed? Why do so many companies fail year after year with their strategies? Why are companies struggling with unmet expectations due to their inability to execute their strategy? Why do we have so many strategic failures? The answer lies in the inability of these companies to brutally confront their realities and accurately diagnose the real obstacles to their progress.

Defining Reality

There are two types of realities companies must confront to develop great strategies and successfully execute them. They are their *internal realities* and their *external realities.* Over the years, I have found that very few business leaders and executives have the capability, emotional fortitude, and managerial courage to brutally confront their internal and external realities. Unfortunately, failure to confront these realities is the major reason why strategy fails with alarming regularity. Even though most organizations and even individuals struggle to grasp the concept, reality is what it is. It is neither good nor bad. It is just what is. And the worst thing that business leaders can do when they get together to craft their strategy is to hide from the truth of their reality. To do this will be tantamount to jumping off a skyscraper with a faulty parachute and hoping to God that somewhere along the way, somehow, the holes in the parachute will fill themselves out and ensure safe landing. But having hope alone has never been a good strategy.

The most important thing in strategy formulation is the accurate diagnosis of the current reality. So, whether you are crafting your organization's strategy, or your personal career strategy, understand that your first and most important responsibility is to identify the biggest challenges to your forward progress and devise a coherent approach to overcoming them. A good strategy must be grounded in reality! It must brutally factor in the challenges being faced and provide an approach or a solution to conquer them. And the bigger the challenge, the more a good strategy must focus and rally its efforts to deliver a powerful and competitive punch to eliminate it. Any strategy that overlooks and shies away from troublesome details will glaringly turn out to be ineffective, always proving to be a complete waste of time.

The same principle applies to strategy execution. The most important factor in strategy execution is to assess the availability of the right resources. This step also must be deeply rooted in unquestionable reality. In the end, successfully scaling the reality hurdle is the key to long term success.

And foundational to achieving significant success is the ability to avoid the always-present, ever-tempting world of delusions. It is very important to guard against self-delusion because confronting reality does not come easy to most of us. It is uncomfortable. Truth can be harsh, and we humans have a natural tendency to gravitate away from pain and towards more pleasure. However, the higher the price we pay in identifying and overcoming our biggest hurdles, the greater the benefits we reap. The reward of a superior perception of reality is high because the better your grasp of reality, the better the quality of your results. The better your results, the better the quality of your life or business.

In his book *Good Strategy/Bad Strategy*, Richard P. Rumelt argued that a good strategy has, at a minimum, three essential components: a diagnosis of the situation, the choice of an overall guiding policy, and the design of coherent action. And I agree with him. We will all do well to get the first component right: accurately diagnosing the situation. As it is with doctors, so it is with strategists. Any doctor will tell you that the most crucial step toward finding a cure is first having the right diagnosis. If a disease is accurately diagnosed, a good resolution is far more likely. Equally, a bad diagnosis usually means a bad outcome, no matter how skilled the physician or strategist may be.

Key Takeaways

- Contrary to one of the biggest myths about the concept of strategy being complex or complicated, strategy is a very simple concept.

- Individuals and organizations that get strategy right understand that they can only effectively articulate a powerful winning strategy when they accurately answer these four distinct questions:

  i. Where are we? - Point A
  ii. Where do we want to go? - Point B
  iii. How do we get there?
  iv. What obstacles must we overcome to close the gap between Point A and Point B?

- Strategy emerges all by itself after accurately answering these questions. Strategy, therefore, is the 'solution' arrived at to close the identified gap between Point A and Point B.

- Many people and businesses fail year after year with their strategies because they do not brutally confront their internal and external realities, accurately diagnose the real obstacles to their progress, and design strategies to address those obstacles.

- Reality is what is, it is neither good nor bad. And the worst thing that business leaders can do when they assemble to craft their strategy is to hide from the truth of their reality. The most important thing in strategy formulation is accurate diagnosis of your reality.

- The same principle applies to strategy execution. It is very important to assess the availability of the right resources in strategy execution.

- The only way to achieve significant success is to guard against self-delusion as confronting reality does not come easy to most of us. It is uncomfortable, truth can be harsh, and we humans have a natural tendency to gravitate towards less pain and more pleasure.

CHAPTER 14

HOW WILL YOU PLAY THE SECOND HALF OF YOUR GAME?

"How you respond to the challenge in the second half will determine what you become after the game, whether you are a winner or a loser."

- Lou Holtz

One of the greatest loves in my life is the game of football. And though this is not much of a secret, especially to my close associates, what is under the radar, however, is the degree of my passion for the game. It is a 'for better or for worse, in good times and in bad times' kind of relationship that is sometimes too intense for my own good. When my team is winning, I am over the moon. When they are losing, I am in a depth of despair that is just plain irrational. Though this chapter has nothing to do with my irrational, bordering on obsessive love for football, it focuses on one of the most important lessons I have learnt from watching the sport that I love so much. The lesson I am referring to is *'How to Play the Second Half of your Game'* be it in sport, career, business, or in life.

In any life endeavor, there always comes a time when you get to the half-way point of whatever you are focusing your efforts on. It could be living one day successfully; in which case the half time is midday. Or working towards a successful week where the midpoint would be Wednesday. Or if you are working towards a successful year, it would be how you would play from July to December. Ultimately, if you are one of those few great souls who keep their eyes constantly on the bigger picture, and are committedly pursuing a specific lifetime goal, if you hope to live until about age 90, and you are now 45 years old, the question then becomes, how do you play the second half of your 90 years on earth?

It is an extremely powerful question to ask yourself because whatever your venture, it is always a game of two halves, much like football. After you have played the first half of your 'game', take out time to 'catch your breath', evaluate your progress and re-strategize for the second half of your 'game'. Doing so increases your probability for long-term success if you are already doing well. If not, neglecting to retreat to the 'dressing room' to evaluate and re-strategize objectively and methodically for better performance, might spell doom for that venture.

Yet, as critical as this half-time evaluation is, only a few people I know of deeply consider it, and until relatively recently, I was equally guilty of doing the same to my own detriment. Fortunately for me, I eventually found that to live unintentionally is to live sub-standardly. And if this is not a tragic way to live, I am not sure what is. How can we ever *be* better, *do* better and *get* better results, if we simply take each day, each month, and each year as it comes, with no plan to assess our (lack of) progress, make necessary adjustments and course correct? Without a doubt, I am convinced that living unconsciously is the reason why many people fail in their endeavors.

People do not fail because they have bad luck working against them. They fail because they successfully resist evaluating their progress by answering the very important question of how they would play their second halves as they go through life. Leaving life to chance is a poor choice and is the main cause of untold suffering, persistent failure, and stagnation in the lives of millions of people. For these people, the tide never seems to turn, nor do things change for the better for them.

So, why do more people not ask, answer and act on this question? Having been guilty of the same thing, here are my top four reasons for failing to ask and effectively answer this question in the past. I reckon that you might relate to these as well.

Reason 1: Discouragement

Let's face it. It takes a special kind of faith to persist in the face of discouragement, especially the kind that arises when the results of the first half of your venture are extremely underwhelming compared to the efforts you put in. For me, discouragements always arose internally and externally. Discouragement from within arose from my very high hopes and the assumption that I could not lose. I discussed my remedy for averting this kind of discouragement in the lesson on the *Principle of Next* (see Chapter 7). On the other hand, my external discouragement typically came from 'members of the discouragement committee' (see Chapter 25), or from external factors that were completely beyond my control.

Either way, the old saying that, when there is a will, there is always a way, is eternally true. So, if I were to give you a solid piece of advice for contending with discouragements—both internal and external—I would say, *just cross the Rubicon.* Another way to say it is to go all in! When you are all in, you are fully committed to your dreams. You are no longer weighing the pros and cons of your goals and objectives. Instead, you direct all your energies to figuring out how to make them a reality.

Reason 2: Hope

A second reason why I buried my head in the sand, rather than face reality and plan on how to do better, was because I was relying on the hope that things would get better by themselves in the second half. In the end, the 'hope strategy' has always let me down.

Reason 3: Overconfidence

The belief that I possessed greater knowledge or skill in tackling future business challenges than I really did, always turned out to be wrong. This infection of overconfidence always overtook me when the first half of my ventures went very well. Arrogance set in, and I underestimated what it took to win in the second half.

Reason 4: Know-how

This always manifested in two ways for me. One, I grossly underestimated the critical importance of preparing for the second half. And two, I had no idea about how to successfully prepare for the second half.

As excusable as these reasons may be, they robbed me of many successes. Whenever I failed to answer the question of how to best play the second half of my game, I lost the opportunity to do better and to get better results. Thankfully, I did not maintain this self-defeating position for too long. After several hard knocks, I came around, and drew from the wisdom that my beloved sport had previously taught me. I learnt to ask and answer what I now consider the ultimate winning question.

And so, the rest of this chapter contains the strategy I have learnt over the years on how to effectively answer the question, **how will you play the second half of your game?** But before I discuss that, I would like to share the event that brought me this wisdom.

The Miracle of Dammam

It was a Saturday, the date was 25th February 1989, and the football game that illuminated my understanding of what great re-evaluation and re-strategization could do to reverse a very bad situation was the match between the USSR and Nigeria. That awe-inspiring match has since been nicknamed *The Miracle of Dammam*.

In what I have come to classify as one of the worst football watching experiences I have ever had, by the time the half-time whistle was blown by the referee, my team, the Nigerian side, was losing 4 – 0 to the USSR team. I was devastated because I found that score very difficult to accept. I was watching the match in my house with friends, and we all agreed that there was absolutely no point in watching the second half. So, we activated emotional damage control, switching off the TV as the second half was about to resume.

Some minutes into the second half, one of my friends that decided to still follow the match on his portable radio announced with a jubilant shout that our team had just scored a goal! In celebration, we all rushed back to the living room and switched on the TV in time to catch a replay of our first goal against the USSR. The score line was now 4 – 1. We debated amongst ourselves and decided that it was still an impossible task to overcome such a huge deficit, not to mention the possibility of the other team scoring more goals. We opted to switch off the TV again, with the hope that perhaps our team would score another goal and at least half the deficit. A few minutes later, our team scored their second goal of the night. Again, we responded to the celebration of my friend who was still listening on the radio by rushing to switch on the TV again in time to watch the replay. At this point, we concluded that somehow, our act of switching off the TV was helping our team (yeah, I know, that sounds irrational, right?) So, we switched off the TV again and repeated the same process until we not only equalized but won the match in a spectacular fashion. It was an unforgettable football match and a truly glorious day for me!

Though this football match took place 32 years ago, till date I still have goose bumps whenever I recount the event. Not only did the experience remain engraved in my mind, but it also became a major source of inspiration for me over the years, serving as a reminder of the ever-present possibility of snatching success from the jaws of defeat. There are different versions of the story of what the coach said to the team during the half time break that sparked the unforgettable comeback. Whatever the facts are, the most important thing I want you to take away from the experience is the gift of inspiration. It is a powerful story of what is possible even with a very rough first half.

And now, let us try to answer the question of how to effectively play the second half.

How to play the second half of your 'game'

In 1905, philosopher George Santayana in his notable work, *The Life of Reason,* wrote, "Those who cannot remember the past are condemned to repeat it." The instruction for us is simple. If we will create a powerful game plan for the second half, we must necessarily **do business with the past!**

To do business with the past is to deeply harvest it for the key *insights* and *lessons* that it holds. Like George Santayana wisely noted, this is the only way to keep ourselves from repeating the mistakes that brought us failure. When you do business with the past, it helps you to uncover the areas where you succeeded and areas where you had significant gaps. Bottlenecks and opportunities for improvements always reveal themselves from a position of hindsight. Analyzing the past helps you discover what works and what doesn't, especially what works, because you do not want to 'fix' what is not broken. And perhaps, what is most important is that dealing with the past helps you to clear your mind and make room for the new. It helps you declutter your memories to better prepare for the future.

When I do business with the past, I use a comprehensive four-step gameplan that is designed to help me achieve an accurate overview of all the insights and lessons that the past has to offer me. This plan enables me to analyze the past, the present and the future, so that when I am done, I would have successfully mined the wisdom of the past, found the gaps in my present and built a strong map to navigate the vicissitudes of the future.

The Four-Step Gameplan

To illustrate how the template works, let's assume that we are working with a yearly agenda. The first six months are over, and so we are now faced with planning how to best play the next six months.

Step 1:
Pride and Regret

1-YEAR GAMEPLAN DESIGNED FOR _____ DESIGNED BY _____ DATE _____

PAST 1-YEAR	PRESENT	FUTURE
I'm proud of...	*I'm confident in...*	*I'm excited about...*
I regret...	*I lack...*	*I worry about...*

Focus Five: What must happen in the next 90 days for you to feel more pride, confidence, and excitement?

This step is structured to enable you to assess the Past. In the Pride column, you answer these key questions: *What have I done and accomplished between January and June that I am most proud of?* After filling in this column, you move to the Regret column and answer similar questions: *What do I regret not doing? What should I have done but haven't that I deeply regret?* Capture these in detail in the Regret column.

While filling these columns, please note that it is very important to objectively capture what has truly worked and what hasn't. A lot of people, especially those that are critical, tend to focus on just the negatives. It is unhealthy to focus excessively on your regrets. In the same way, there are those who are too focused on the positives, ignoring the areas for correction. The only way to successfully play the second half better is to balance both sides out—your prides and your regrets. Contrary to what many people think, regrets are okay, if they are viewed as opportunities to begin anew, and this time more intelligently, just as Henry Ford advised. So, it is very important to not allow your regrets to become shackles that hold you down. Instead, use them as a force to propel you to achieve greater heights. Whenever I review my first half regrets, I direct my emotional energies from one of discouragement to anger and use this anger to challenge myself to do better.

Step 2:
Confidence and Lack

1-YEAR GAMEPLAN   DESIGNED FOR _____ DESIGNED BY _____ DATE _____

PAST 1-YEAR	PRESENT	FUTURE
I'm proud of...	I'm confident in...	I'm excited about...
I regret...	I lack...	I worry about...

Focus Five: What must happen in the next 90 days for you to feel more pride, confidence, and excitement?

This aspect of the game plan is designed to enable you analyze the **Present.** In this section, you must answer the questions: *In this present time, what do I have working for me? What am I confident in and what do I presently lack?*

When I consult for businesses, I always encourage them to answer these questions in detail because it helps to shed light on those critical factors that will help them stay on track in meeting their goals. It is very important to assess what makes you feel confident in the present and what you lack that makes you feel unsure and undermines your sense of assurance of winning. These are very important variables to consider because in the areas where you are confident, you can do more and add effort to improve it. Wherever you have identified some lack, you would need to zoom in on it to establish what you need to do differently to get better results.

Step 3:
Excitement and Worry

1-YEAR GAMEPLAN   DESIGNED FOR _____   DESIGNED BY _____   DATE _____

PAST 1-YEAR	PRESENT	FUTURE
I'm proud of...	I'm confident in...	I'm excited about...
I regret...	I lack...	I worry about...

Focus Five: What must happen in the next 90 days for you to feel more pride, confidence, and excitement?

This step addresses some part of the **Future**. In assessing the next half of the year, you must first identify what really makes you excited. Ask and answer the question: *What am I looking forward to in the next half of the year?* After doing this, identify what makes you feel worried. Articulate these concerns clearly.

Step 4:
Future Focus

1-YEAR GAMEPLAN   DESIGNED FOR _____   DESIGNED BY _____   DATE _____

PAST 1-YEAR	PRESENT	FUTURE
I'm proud of...	I'm confident in...	I'm excited about...
I regret...	I lack...	I worry about...

Focus Five: What must happen in the next 90 days for you to feel more pride, confidence, and excitement?

This step asks very powerful questions: *What must happen in the next 6 months for me to feel more proud, confident, and excited? What must I do to have less regrets, less lack and less worry? What must happen?* This is where the plan comes in. When you look at what you are proud of and confident in, ask yourself: *How do I do more of that? How can I create more of what makes me excited?* And then ask yourself: *How do I reduce what causes regret, lack and worry?*

So, it boils down to an 'Improve and Reduce' grid. *How do I reduce the number of things that I regret? How do I reduce the number of things that I lack (it could be knowledge, support, time, or something else)? And how do I reduce the number of things that worry me?*

You can download a copy of your personal gameplan template from www. ownersinstitute.com. The template is adjustable to allow you evaluate and re-strategize for the second half of your day, your week, your month, your year, or even a batch of years.

If you use the gameplan template properly, you should be able to accurately answer the following questions:

- What were some wins in the first half?

- What are the obvious bottlenecks?

- What are the big opportunities?

- What are the lessons learned?

Asking and answering these questions complete the process. The next step is to assess and act. And this way you can end up creating a dependable game plan to effectively play your second half.

Key Takeaways

- Asking and answering the question: 'How to Play the Second Half of your Game', whether it be sport, career, business, or life, is one of the most important lessons I have learnt.

- In any endeavor in life, you will always get to the half-way point of the focus of your efforts. It could be living one day successfully, in which case the half time is midday, or living a successful life, in which case the midpoint would depend upon how long you want to live.

- When you get to the midpoint of your endeavor, it is crucial to ask yourself the question: How am I going to play the second half of my game?

- This question is crucial because after you have played the first half of your 'game', taking out time to evaluate your progress and re-strategizing for the second half, increases your probability for long-term success if you are already doing well. If you are not doing well, neglecting to retreat to the 'dressing room' to evaluate your performance and re-strategizing objectively and methodically for better performance, might spell doom for whatever your venture is.

- But many people neglect to ask and act on this question for the following reasons.

  i. They are overwhelmed by the discouragement from failures in the first half.
  ii. They hope that things will work themselves out.
  iii. They become overconfident in their ability to tackle the second half effortlessly.
  iv. They do not appreciate how crucial it is to plan for the second half of their 'game'. And even when they do, they do not know how to successfully plan for the second half.

- If we will succeed in creating a powerful game plan for the second half, we must necessarily do business with the past, by deeply harvesting its key insights and lessons.

- When I do business with the past, I use a comprehensive four-step gameplan template that is designed to help me achieve an accurate overview of all the insights and lessons that the past has to offer me. The template is attached for your use.

CHAPTER 15

EXECUTION: THE SOLE DETERMINANT OF SUCCESS AND FAILURE

"Vision without execution is hallucination."
- Thomas Edison

One of the most heart-breaking statements of fact that I have ever heard was uttered by Les Brown. He said, "The graveyard is the richest place on earth, because it is here that you will find all the hopes and dreams that were never fulfilled, the books that were never written, the songs that were never sung, the inventions that were never shared, the cures that were never discovered, all because someone was too afraid to take that first step, keep with the problem, or determined to carry out their dream."

I honestly do not believe that anyone can overemphasize the fact that success or failure is not a matter of luck, circumstance, fate, connections, or any of the thousand other excuses that some people give to justify their lack of achievement. Success in any venture at all is a matter of following the principles and laws that have been proven to produce that outcome, the chief of these principles being EXECUTION.

As a case in point, a landmark study of the top weight loss programmes in the world revealed three very interesting facts:

1. All the programmes worked.

2. They worked only when people used them as prescribed.

3. People rarely used them as prescribed if they used them at all.

Would *Ali Baba* have revolutionized Jack Ma's life if he had not taken one step after another in pursuing the birth of the online marketplace?

The answer to this question is obvious, and so is the fact that the great tragedy of many people and many businesses is not that they lack good ideas, or that they **have a knowledge gap. What unsuccessful individuals and businesses have is an execution problem, that is, the discipline of acting on what they know.** The discipline of execution is crucial to success in life and business because it is implementation, and not ideas that determines success.

At this point, I must say something about the widely accepted thought that *ideas rule the world.* This is not exactly accurate. In themselves, ideas are powerless, no matter how innovative or fantastic they appear to be. On their own, unassisted by hard work and brilliant execution, ideas cannot make anyone successful any more than thinking about driving a car gets the car moving. Just as you need to turn on the ignition and press on the accelerator to get a car moving, so also must you break your brilliant ideas into actionable steps and follow through to execute them into reality. And for most individuals and organizations, this is where the problem lies.

Minding the Execution Gap

It is said that the greatest gap in life is the one between knowing and doing. Far too many people talk more about doing, than do what they talk about. Unfortunately, as long as the scale is tipped in this way, such people will continue to experience little to no progress.

Take a moment to think about your definition of success and identify those who you consider successful. I am absolutely convinced that every single successful person you can think of is a doer, an action-biased individual. And so, your responsibility is to do everything possible to bridge the gap between knowing and doing, between talking and acting out your talk. You must do whatever it takes to close this gap, because you can be very talented, smart, and knowledgeable, and it would not matter one ounce. What the marketplace rewards is doing, not just knowing. It is what you do with what you know that counts.

So, whether it is a new year resolution, a career growth initiative, revenue driven objective, business expansion or customer acquisition and retention plans, you must fully recognize that hitting those set targets will require a lot more than planning and strategizing. It will require deliberate action. To guarantee your career success or business survival, you must become comfortable alternating between the two creative phases: ideation and execution.

To avoid making the mistakes that most people make, you must also contemplate the question of why *many individuals and companies never succeed in making the successful transition from drafting to actualizing their goals. Why do so many individuals and organizations alike never succeed in translating their well-articulated vision and mission statements, strategies, goals, and great plans into tangible achievements?*

*From my y*ears of trying to answer this question, I have come to realize that there are two main reasons behind this trend: a lack of effective and consistent review of their set goals, and a lack of a suitable accountability partner.

From the first point, regularly reviewing your set goals is the hallmark of the discipline of getting things done. Consistency of results is practically impossible without regular reviews. Successful companies attribute their continued success to effective and consistent monthly/quarterly/annual performance reviews (MPR/QPR/APR).

Personally, I have my version of reviewing my goals and I call it *BPR – Bolaji's Performance Review*. To keep myself on top of things, I carry out this review on a weekly basis. The process of my BPR is rather simple, as illustrated next.

Step 1: A review of what I planned to do in the just concluded week.

Step 2: A score of what I was able to achieve.

Step 3: A written account of why I under-achieved on any goal, if any, and what I learned.

Step 4: A plan for course correction.

Step 5: A detailed plan for the new week/month.

If you apply the steps in my BPR, and do it consistently, you will see a remarkable difference in your results. Doing this over time will help to further develop and grow your execution intelligence.

Before we discuss the lack of a suitable accountability partner, kindly take a moment to ponder these questions:

- How far would you like to go in life, your career or business?
- How badly would you like to accelerate your career growth or business results?
- How intense is your desire for spectacular success?
- How hungry are you for extraordinary achievements?

Here is how to manifest these powerful desires in your life: Be accountable to someone for your plans, your commitments, and your results.

The higher you want to go or the better the things you want to get, the greater the requirement to have someone in your life who will hold you accountable and tell you the brutal truth.

It is a major mistake to assume that you do not need an accountability partner to achieve your goals. I am very convinced that this assumption will prove fatal to achieving your dreams and aspirations because I know first-hand that our brains are simply too powerful at making excuses and creating elaborate justifications for why we did not get something important done or did not follow through on a task.

The hard truth is that we make promises to ourselves, but we also tend to break them with alarming regularity. *For some reason, the promises we make to ourselves are less sacred than the promises we make to others.* Therefore, the only way to realistically evade this execution landmine is to have a respected accountability partner who will hold you to your commitments. This is a crucial ingredient to making sustainable progress for success.

When you eventually decide to get an accountability partner, be very sure that it is someone you trust to tell you the truth. This person must be someone who will not buy into your cheap excuses for why you fell off the wagon or did not get the job done, someone who has the courage to tell you "No!"

And if you find yourself thinking that you know no one who fits the bill of a worthy accountability partner, remember that *the man or woman who really wants to do something always finds a way; the others find excuses.*

In solving this problem for myself, I hired a coach to hold me accountable for achieving my goals. Yes! You read that right. Her responsibility is to make sure I do what I am supposed to do, whether I feel like it or not. To raise the stakes, part of our contract is that I will pay her double her fees at the end of every quarter if I do not achieve 75% of my big goals. This makes me extremely motivated to do whatever it takes because her services are not cheap.

You see, my dreams are just too big to leave to my own clever excuses and the ingenious reasons I can easily come up with to avoid doing what I am supposed to do, when I am supposed to do it.

The difference in the quality of my life and business before and after hiring an accountability coach are not only massive, but they are also extremely measurable.

For instance, before I hired my accountability coach, I kept saying that I would write a book every year over a period of 10 years. But year after year, I consistently failed to achieve this feat. For the past two years since I have hired an accountability coach, I have written 2 books, and this is now my 3rd book. I am absolutely convinced that I could not have done this without paying someone to follow up on me and hold me accountable.

In life, you are either creating desirable circumstances for yourself by executing your plans and strategies, or you are creating undesirable circumstances for yourself by stalling, over-analyzing your strategies and over-polishing your business plans to the point of paralysis. The only true way forward is to do something. When you act, there will always be a reaction. You can always adjust your actions to get better reactions, if you do not like the reactions that you get at first. It is this constant cycle of action and reaction that begets success. However, if you do not act, nothing happens.

The question then is, are you going to become accountable for delivering results, or will you continue delivering excuses? Moreover, to what extent are you willing to go to turn your dreams into a reality?

Nothing will change your life faster than developing the discipline of getting things done—the discipline of execution. It is practically impossible to overstate the importance of this ability. Nothing will hasten your success faster than disciplining yourself to give yourself orders and obeying them!

So, with all thy getting, get great at getting things done. The benefits to you will be unquantifiable.

Key Takeaways

- Success or failure is not a matter of luck, circumstance, fate, connections, or any of the many other excuses that some people give to justify their lack of achievement. Success in any venture is a matter of following the principles and laws that have been proven to produce that outcome. The chief of these principles is EXECUTION.

- The great tragedy of many people and businesses is not that they lack good ideas, or relevant knowledge. What unsuccessful individuals and businesses have is an execution problem: the discipline of acting on what they know. The discipline of execution is crucial to success in life and business because it is implementation, and not ideas that determine success.

- Ideas do not necessarily rule the world. On their own without hard-work and brilliant execution, ideas cannot make anyone successful any more than thinking about driving a car can get the car moving.

- The greatest gap in life is the one between knowing and doing. Far too many people talk more about doing, than doing what they talk about. If the scale remains so unbalanced, such people will continue to experience little or no progress.

- Successful people are doers, they are action-biased individuals. Your responsibility is to do everything possible to bridge the gap between knowing and doing, the gap between talking and acting on your talk.

- Many individuals and companies never succeed in making the successful transition from their drafted goals to actualized goals for two reasons:
  i. Lack of effective and consistent review of their set goals.
  ii. Lack of an Accountability Partner.

- In life, you are either creating desirable circumstances for yourself by executing your plans and strategies, or undesirable circumstances for yourself by stalling and over-analyzing your strategies to the point of paralysis.

- The only true way forward is to do something. When you act, there will always be a reaction. You can always adjust your actions to get better reactions. It is this constant cycle of action-reaction that begets success.

CHAPTER 16

THE MYSTERY OF MASTERY

"If a man can write a better book or preach a better sermon or make a better mousetrap than his neighbor, even if he builds his house in the woods, the world will make a beaten path to his door."

- Ralph Waldo Emerson

I have always had a very strong desire to be a success right from when I was very young. I wanted to succeed so badly that I was willing to do anything morally right. So naturally, I chased hard after success. Very hard. As far back as I can remember, my every waking moment was spent doing one thing or another that I thought would enable me to succeed. If I read a book, it was about how to be successful. If I volunteered for a cause, I did it because I hoped to gain some success recipe or advantage out of it. Everything I remember doing as a young child, a teenager and an adult was success-driven. Needless to say, success was an obsession.

However, at some point, it became obvious to me that the more I tried, the more elusive my grand pursuit of success seemed to become. Do not get me wrong, I was doing okay, at least well enough to meet my needs. But I wanted so much more, and the struggle was real. The level of success I wanted, that I had spent years dreaming of, far exceeded what I had achieved so far, and every day the gap between my vision of success and my achievements widened to the extent that frustration began to set in.

Then, one fateful day, one fortuitous and extremely profound conversation with a colleague and friend changed everything. It is said that success is not necessarily a product of one isolated, momentous event, but a series of small, consistent, and powerful actions. Be that as it may, whenever I look back, I am pretty sure that but for this illuminating conversation with my friend, I would not have acquired the idea that birthed the change in my thinking, my disposition, and my subsequent results. At the risk of sounding melodramatic, I dare say that that conversation with my friend which I am about to relate to you not only changed my attitude to life, but it also changed my entire philosophy about success and what it means to be truly successful.

My friend and colleague, who was a full-time consultant, and a part-time pastor came to my office and said that he had discovered something while studying his Bible, a discovery that he believed was "The Secret to Sustained Success".

My first inclination was to roll my eyes and crack my long-standing joke, in which I called him an accidental consultant and asked him to fully go after his true calling, which was to be a Christian Minister. However, my friend remained serious, and the pensive look on his face and his demeanor— like he had just had a spiritual encounter—stopped me from making light of his remarks. I am sure glad I stopped kidding around because unknown to me, I was about to learn something truly remarkable. I asked him to sit down and share what he had learnt with me, but he declined insisting that he would rather stand. Then he walked over to the flip chart stand in my office and wrote this Bible verse:

2 Timothy 2:5: "And if a man also strives for masteries, yet is he not crowned; except he strives lawfully…"

After he wrote this out, he completely blew my mind with 7 distinct Principles of Mastery that he had drawn from this very deep verse. Even though I recall much of the profound charge he gave that day, I will keep the key principles short and to the point.

Principle 1: In every field or endeavor, there are those who are considered as Masters.

Principle 2: To qualify as a true MASTER, one must be crowned. Therefore, a crown is the only proof that one has mastered something. A crown signifies *royalty, wealth, influence, and authority*. No matter the shape or title they come in, all these are natural by-products of having achieved MASTERY.

Principle 3: There is only one way to attain MASTERY of anything, and that is through well-calculated and sustained effort or striving. Mastery is not a function of genius or talent or luck. It is a function of time and intensely well-applied **focus** on a particular field of **knowledge**. You must strive to achieve mastery.

Principle 4: It is very possible to strive long and hard but still fail to achieve mastery and the desired reward if you do not know how to strive correctly.

Principle 5: There are systematic laws and principles guiding how we must strive.

Not to follow these specific laws is to run the risk of striving but not achieving the desired results. These laws must be learnt and followed dutifully if we are to get those results. If you desire mastery, you can never be crowned as a master until you learn to live by the laws that lead to mastery.

Principle 6: Every single human being is a completely unique creation. Therefore, as a human being, you have unlimited potential, and you can attain masteries in different endeavors.

Principle 7: In summary, to achieve high level success in life, you must first identify a high impact area to play in. Next, practice deliberately to develop exceptional abilities in those areas, and then lastly, run hard and diligently in the prescribed way to receive the crown.

These are Powerful Principles! Absolutely Powerful!!

There is a saying that when the student is ready, the teacher will appear. That fateful morning, I was ready, my teacher appeared, and I got thoroughly educated. I got the message loud and clear. When Benjamin Disraeli said there is no education like adversity, I am convinced that he meant that we all tend to learn best from what is painful. For some reason, as a species, our deepest and greatest education rises from areas where we have faced great struggles and challenges.

These principles that my friend shared with me may appear straightforward and common-sensical, but after struggling without their light for very long, the entrance of their wisdom was heralded with great fanfare in my soul. I embraced them, understood them, and worked them at a level much deeper than what most people may have chosen to do. And so far, they have deeply rewarded me.

From the exact day that I sat through that conversation until this day, my focus shifted from the pursuit of success to the pursuit of mastery. I stopped asking questions like, *How can I achieve success?* And I began to ask questions like, *What do I need to master to guarantee success?*

The Vault of Success

A lot of people are trying to open the vault of success without its key. The key to the vault holding yours or anyone's success is Mastery. And the key to mastery is effort. Too many people believe that everything must be effortless in life, viewing effort as a sign that something is wrong and consequently, pulling away from it. This is the main reason behind the shortage of achievement in our world today—too many people pull away from pain and effort. They run and hide from anything that tasks their minds, hands, and hearts, choosing instead to inundate themselves with the unending pursuit of pleasure. They find pleasure alright, however, it is short-lived. And the sting behind this pleasure is that it camouflages a lifetime of pain and discomfort. Therefore, I say, do not pursue comfort; pursue mastery, it will bring comfort.

Mastery is attainable for all

Everyone can attain mastery in any field or endeavor they choose. Although I know this for a fact, I also know that nobody gets good at anything without lots of deliberate practice and repetition. Most people do not possess any kind of mastery not because they lack the capacity for it, but because they are satisfied to live in their comfort zone and never do the work that is required to get out of it and make for themselves a remarkable life. They prefer to live in the world of 'good enough.' Unfortunately, the land called 'good enough' never remains good enough for long enough.

Rid yourself of the barriers to mastery

Even though we all can attain mastery, two things keep most people away from this glorious attainment. One, the preference of comfort over the discomfort of attaining mastery. Two, impatience with the process of attaining mastery.

When you really think about the first barrier, the love of comfort, there is nothing comfortable about a comfort zone. Eventually you will become stagnant and stranded. The difficulties of attaining mastery are temporary but lead to glory. The difficulties of the comfort-zone induced problems are endless, leading to a life of misery. Choose wisely.

As for the second barrier to achieving mastery, please understand that mastery cannot be rushed, it is a journey. It requires *many hours of dedicated focus and practice*. You cannot attain mastery if your work brings you no joy. It therefore becomes imperative to select an area for mastery carefully. Many paths can lead you to mastery if you work the principles. My advice is, find a sweet spot, that is, an area that suits your strengths and stick to it.

Mastery is the only key to long-term success

A major reason to pursue mastery is the fact that success can breed complacency and there are chances that you can end up losing the success you have created if you fall back into your comfort zone. I have observed people succeed in an area, become comfortable, drop the habits of success, and lose that success. This observation sobers me up and keeps me on my toes. The wisdom I take from such cases is to never stop pursuing mastery.

To stop pushing the boundaries of mastery is to enter a phase of decline. The moment you rest, thinking that you have arrived, a part of your mind enters the first phase of 'decay', and decline starts automatically. The pursuit of mastery must therefore be continually followed. I would be lying if I said that the path to mastery was easy, it is not. But despite how challenging it is, the beautiful thing about mastery is that no one can take it from you. Once the flywheel of mastery starts rolling, you can always rebuild and recreate your successes.

If for whatever reason, attaining mastery in any field remains out of your reach, please make sure you achieve mastery in the areas of how you spend your time, how you use your money, and how you cultivate and maintain the right relationships. These are non-negotiables as far as success in life is concerned.

PS: In the past when I have shared about the power of mastery, I have had many people come up to me to say that the entire concept of mastering a subject to attain success and significance is simple and unoriginal. My response to them is, such is the nature of whatever is of eternal truth. Eternal truths are hardly ever complex. Nature does not do mankind the injustice of complicating important things. So, embrace this simple idea of mastery and take it seriously, it will make all the difference in your life.

I leave you with the words of Martin Luther King Jr. "Be a bush if you can't be a tree. If you can't be a highway, just be a trail. If you can't be a sun, be a star. For it isn't by size that you win or fail. Be the best of whatever you are."

Key Takeaways

In every field or endeavor, there are those who are considered Masters. The key to the vault holding your success or anyone's success for that matter is mastery, and the key to mastery is effort.

Don't pursue comfort. Pursue mastery, it will bring comfort.

Anyone can attain mastery in their field. The reason that most people don't possess any kind of mastery is not because they lack the capacity for it, but because they prefer comfort. They shy away from doing the work that is required to attain mastery.

A major reason to pursue mastery is that success can breed complacency and there are chances of losing the success you have created if you fall back into your comfort zone. I have observed people succeed in an area, become comfortable, drop the habits of success, and then lose that success.

If for whatever reason, attaining mastery in any field remains out of your reach, please make sure you achieve mastery in how you spend your time, use your money, and cultivate and maintain the right relationships. These are non-negotiables as far as success in life is concerned.

CHAPTER 17

THE MOST EFFECTIVE STRATEGY I KNOW FOR BEATING THE ODDS AND SUCCEEDING IN BUSINESS & CAREER

"The average person puts about 25% of his energy and ability into his work. The world takes its hat off to those who put more than 50% of their capacity into their work, and the world stands on its head for those few and far between souls who devote 100%."

- Andrew Carnegie

Why do people get stuck? What causes people to lose momentum and experience decline in their business or career? And what can you do to keep from getting stuck, facing decline, or losing momentum?

I have always been deeply curious about the patterns in human behavior that give rise to various outcomes. And so, when I began to ponder the question of what caused people to come to a gridlock in their careers and businesses, my inquisitive mind went into overdrive in x-raying my personal experiences and those of several others who I have coached and mentored. Through the processes of personal introspection and observation of others, it became more and more obvious that one key reason why people, including me, find themselves stuck in seemingly intractable career, business or life problems is that they stop taking ownership of their personal learning, growth, and development.

Believe me when I tell you that this is in no way a theoretical or hasty assumption. I have experienced this situation time and time again and as an ardent observer of myself and others, this pattern of '*zero personal development = zero progress*' has played out all too frequently to permit its dismissal as mere chance or coincidence.

At this point, allow me to advise that if you will ever defy the odds that are stacked against you in life, career and business, the best place to launch out from is to first develop the profound habit of studying yourself. If you master the art of stepping outside of yourself to watch your own actions and reactions like an external observer, you will begin to learn about your 'blind spots' and the 'danger zones' that have the potential to devastate your progress.

For instance, I have observed that whenever I start something new and I am eager to make it a success, I start learning everything I can on that subject matter. After a while, I start to make progress, and then I learn more and experience more progress. As this cycle continues for a while, during times like these, life is good indeed. However, somewhere along the line, I get into my comfort zone, leaving my learning and personal growth to chance, and because my progress does not stop immediately, I continue this downward trend. And this is where the problem lies. If only the progress I was making grinded to a halt the moment I stopped learning, I doubt that I or most other people with similar experiences would ever stop learning. But this is not the case. It takes a while for the progress I have been making to reach its plateau, and when it does (as it always does) the struggle starts.

And when I fall into this hole, rather than revert to learning, I default to doubling down on my efforts trying to sweat it out or using brute force to restart the progress that I was previously enjoying. There have been times when brute force failed, and I quickly regained my 'senses' and reverted to my learning mode. But for those unfortunate times when my brute efforts or sheer force yielded some progress, my fate was sealed in those moments. It would signal the beginning of a long spell of struggling, groping in the dark and banging my head against the wall in the false hope that more struggles will bring my desired progress.

However, instead of progress, the decline continued. And like quicksand, the more I struggled, the worse it got. It is at this point that the enemies of progress, shrouded as feelings of discouragement, loss of confidence, negativity, etc., start to creep in.

Having experienced quite a number of these periods and cycles, they have marked the darkest times in my life. In some instances, this state of being lasted for very long periods, spiraling out of control to the point of affecting other areas of my life, including my relationships and health. The scenario I have just described is very common indeed, and so, I am not alone in this; I have met hundreds of people that have had similar experiences.

In all of these, what bothers me to no end is our tendency as humans to repeat the same mistake again and again. My theory behind the recurring nature of this joy-stealing, destiny-derailing and unpleasant cycle is that people going through such ordeals are way too close to the issue to stand a chance of detecting what is going on early enough. And early detection allows for early course correction and making the necessary changes before we are neck-deep or buried completely in this self-perpetuating situation.

One of the longest spells I have experienced happened about 6 years ago. It went on for almost 3 years and it was brutal. It almost robbed me of everything I had including my health; it got so bad that I experienced extreme burnout. I had never experienced anything like it before, nor do I wish it on anyone.

If you have ever been in such a situation, below are some of the possible experiences you might have had or are still dealing with.

1. You feel like nobody around you truly understands the depth of what you are going through.

2. You feel like everyone around you expects you to be at your normal 'A Game' even though you are not able to deliver at your very best anymore like you used to.

3. You feel you have over complicated your life/business and do not know how to simplify.

4. You sometimes feel that the solution is to drastically streamline or even quit but you cannot because too much is at stake, and you might lose out on opportunities or suffer consequences which might make things worse.

5. You feel you are trying to do too much yet it seems impossible to cut back and focus.

6. You feel that you desperately need help from people that have walked in your shoes before or have the requisite experience to help you out, but you do not know who these people are nor how to find and engage them.

7. You procrastinate more now than you have ever done in the past.

8. Staying positive and motivated is a daily struggle.

9. You sometimes feel like you are back to your old self only to slip back to feeling stuck in only a matter of days.

10. The light at the end of the tunnel feels farther and farther away.

11. You find it much more difficult than normal to stay a course of action and follow through to the end on your commitments.

12. You are constantly searching for a silver bullet, the one single move that will transform everything around you.

13. To numb the frustration you are feeling, you find yourself watching excessive amounts of TV.

14. Most times, you feel helpless.

15. Despite your efforts, you feel like things are getting worse rather than improving.

16. The things happening around you are gradually making you lose hope of a successful turnaround of your situation.

17. Quitting and giving up feels more appealing.

18. You worry that the value you have created over time will be eroded without you being able to capture some of it back.

19. It feels like you could possibly lose out completely.

20. People around you appear not to have anything at risk and hence cannot appreciate the depth of the issues you are dealing with.

21. If given the opportunity, you feel like you are willing to shut everything down and start all over again.

22. It looks like you are fast running out of time and options.

23. Sometimes, you feel like it is already too late to reverse the tide of things to your advantage.

24. It feels like for every 2 steps you take forward, you end up 5-6 steps backwards.

25. Have you noticed that you have stopped enjoying, or even started to dread doing the very things you used to love doing?

26. You have lost passion for things you used to be so gung-ho about.

27. Because you feel vulnerable, you think people around you are taking advantage of that.

28. But you are almost very certain that there is help out there, if only you could find it.

29. It feels like a struggle to sustain momentum.

30. Networking, building, or maintaining key relationships feels harder.

31. If you were to choose, would you rather be on your own than with other people?

32. Do you feel like you are constantly on a treadmill?

33. Advice from others to slow down and take the time off feels not only unrealistic, but also has the potential to make things worse.

34. If only the people advising you appreciated your context, you feel like they would understand your situation and be able to truly confront your realities.

35. Your mind keeps telling you that if something does not change soon, you stand to lose everything including your mind.

36. Does your life feel like a pendulum swinging between despair and desperation, without respite?

37. Are you experiencing a feeling of being trapped by the decisions you have made in the past or by your business or career?

If some or most of these pointers have been your reality, I know exactly what that feels like as I have been down that path personally. And in coming out on the other side much better and wiser, I found that the key was committing to taking complete and total ownership of my learning and personal growth. This, also, is crucial to getting unstuck and turning around the situation in your life, business, and career. Taking ownership and going to school on your biggest problems or opportunities is the key to getting and staying unstuck.

Now, whenever I start struggling or I start to feel like I am getting stuck in any area of my life or business, I know exactly what to do. The very first thing I do is step back and ask myself these questions.

1. What am I required to know about this situation that I don't and is causing me to struggle?

2. What insights do I lack that is causing my lack of progress?

3. What do I not see in this situation I find myself in that is creating a gap or blind spot?

4. What do I need to learn?

5. From whom or where can I learn it?

6. Who can help?

I have found that once I take ownership of my learning, the first thing I notice is that I start to feel better, despair starts to turn to hope and that creates even more momentum. Sometimes I spend hours, sometimes days or even weeks asking and searching for these answers. How long it takes doesn't matter as long as I find the right answer.

I created the *Owners Institute Platform* (https://ownersinstitute.com/) because I believe with every fiber of my being that the principle of ownership thinking and acting is the solution to most of the challenges we encounter in life. I am so convinced of it that I can boldly say that if you put me in any challenging situation, as long as a solution exists, I can learn my way out of that situation. And so can you too. Anyone who is committed to learning and willing to take complete and total ownership of their learning and personal growth, can.

After nearly twenty years of navigating the turbulent waters of growing a business in one of the toughest economic climates in the world, I have come to realize that one of the most powerful insights that I possess is understanding *what I cannot do*. And what I absolutely cannot do is make or sustain progress in my business without investing heavily in my personal development. It just cannot be done. This understanding keeps me out of the woods, helps me select my battles, navigate my path, and focus my energies. Focusing my energies becomes even more important because time and energy are elements of life that are in finite supply. It is therefore a great tragedy to waste your time and energy in fighting a battle that you cannot win.

"Knowing what you don't know is more useful than being brilliant. Acknowledging what you don't know is the dawning of wisdom."— Charles Munger.

I am not ashamed to say that I have fought and lost many battles against the 'need to keep learning and developing myself'. With both humility and excitement, I admit that if I ever stop learning and developing myself, I will never ever succeed or thrive in my business or career. I am just not gifted enough to make progress by guesswork, and so I don't bother with that strategy. I make progress by having full knowledge of whatever subject matter I engage myself with and deploying this knowledge accurately.

In conclusion, I have found that, like Confucius said, educating myself on my business breeds confidence. Confidence breeds hope. Hope breeds peace. Knowing this has liberated me! And it will do the same for you too.

Key Takeaways

A key reason why people, including me, find themselves stuck in difficult and seemingly intractable career, business or life problems is that they stopped taking ownership of their personal learning and growth.

Master the art of stepping outside of yourself to watch your own actions and reactions like an observer; you will begin to learn about your 'blind spots' and the 'danger zones' that have the potential to hinder your progress.

The key to getting and staying unstuck in life, business, and career is to go to school on your biggest problems or opportunities. Start your learning by asking and answering these six fundamental questions:

i.   What am I required to know about this situation that I don't and is causing me to struggle?
ii.   What insights do I lack that is stopping my progress?
iii. What don't I see in this situation that is creating a gap or blind spot?
iv.   What do I need to learn?
v.   From whom or where can I learn it?
vi.   Who can help?

Anyone who is committed to learning and is willing to take complete and total ownership of their learning and personal growth can learn their way out of any situation.

I created the *Owners Institute Platform* (ownersinstitute.com) to support you because I believe with every fiber in my being that taking ownership is the solution to most of the challenges we encounter in life.

CHAPTER 18

DO THIS IF YOU WANT TO GROW AND ACHIEVE OUTSIZED RESULTS

"If you cannot see where you are going, ask someone who has been there before."

- J Loren Norris

A young professional approached me recently, asking me to tell him *the number one thing* that made all the difference in generating the success that I had achieved in business.

I spoke this one word in response to him: **Mentorship.** My reason for choosing that answer is very simple. I can trace every single achievement of mine to my interaction with mentors. Every single one!

The benefits of having a mentor/coach/advisor cannot be over-emphasized. If you want accelerated progress and success in any area of your life, whether in relationships, career, business, finance or spiritually, get yourself a suitable mentor. And I am convinced that if people heeded this simple advice and found the right mentors for themselves, the degree of accelerated growth they would experience would be nothing short of miraculous.

Something to ponder deeply is the fact that God could have decided to parachute you into the earth when you were born and leave you to sort yourself out. You and I know that He has the power and know-how to do so. But rather than doing this, He orchestrated your birth through your parents. He also physically engineered them to be two. And you know, two (good) heads are better than one.

When you went to school, you had several teachers who understood the subjects better than you did. Your parents sent you to school to learn from them, as opposed to winging it by home-schooling you or leaving it to you to figure it all out for yourself.

When it was time to start driving, you hopefully hired and paid a qualified driving instructor. To learn how to swim, you hired a swimming trainer. When you were ill, you went to the doctor to sort you out. And God forbid, but you will need to hire a lawyer to defend you when you have legal matters to settle.

My question is, why in the world do people fail to employ this same approach to their lives, relationships, careers, or businesses? Why do people neglect to invest in coaches, trainers, mentors, and advisers to help them succeed in life and in business? Why do people fail to seek out relationship counsellors, business coaches and money mentors even when they have crises in these areas? It is completely puzzling to me.

Why do people prefer to feel their way in the dark, making tons of unnecessary and sometimes potentially devastating mistakes without proper guidance, support, or accountability, especially with the most important things in their lives?

Why do people prefer to waste a great deal of time and effort in creating something that already exists?

In life, there is absolutely no need to reinvent the wheel because "success always leaves clues". People who have achieved exceptional success in various areas of their lives succeeded because they did specific things to create those results. After years of observing the patterns of outstanding business performers, I came away with one powerful success clue: *successful people invest continually and significantly in coaches, mentors, and advisors.*

Denzel Washington, one of my all-time favorite actors, could not have said it any better than this, "Show me a successful individual and I'll show you someone who had real positive influences in his or her life. I don't care what you do for a living—if you do it well, I'm sure there was someone cheering you on or showing the way. A mentor."

To have a mentor is to have a brain to pick, an ear that listens, and a push in the right direction. To be mentored is to have someone who has travelled a particular road guide your every step and keep you out of the 'potholes and land mines' that are sure to derail or even devastate you. There is simply no substitute for a good mentor. And one of the most important decisions you can ever make if you want to achieve outsized results in your most crucial endeavors is to get one.

Simply put, **to be the best in the shortest time, you must learn from the best.**

If your goal is to be the best, the logical thing to do is to learn from the best. However, the best people are also the busiest, always busy 'sharpening their saws' and 'claiming new territories'. So, how do you gain access to their wisdom?

For those who genuinely have the desire and drive to succeed, here are the steps to follow to gain access to the best minds:

Step 1
Pick a mentor, coach, or teacher

Find someone who has a lot of experience in something you want to learn and shares a lot about their experiences through media such as books, blogs, videos, social media posts, etc.

Step 2
Read or watch everything they have ever created multiple times

Re-visit their content regularly. Read their social media posts, articles, books, blogs. Watch their videos, attend their seminars, listen to their talks.

Step 3
Put what you have learnt from them into practice

Make sure you practice as often as possible. Remember, nobody gets good at anything without practice and repetition. At the very least, get a notebook or journal and write the summaries of what you have learned. A lot of clarity comes from writing. Also, make sure you are not just learning for learning's sake. You must apply what you have learnt. You must execute!

Step 4
Once you have applied what you have learnt, consider teaching it to others as soon as possible

This helps with retention, and the more you teach, the more you achieve mastery of the subject. It is a universal life principle.

You will eventually imbibe their lessons, outgrow your mentors, or at least pick up the lessons you need and be ready for a new mentor. Once you have learned almost everything this mentor has to teach you, move on to the next mentor. Note that it is wise and highly beneficial to pick one mentor, coach, or teacher at a time. Aim to learn from only one or two individuals at a time, so that you can get the most out of the experience.

Over the years, I have had several mentors in different areas (and I still do). However, very few of these relationships have been formal mentor-mentee or teacher-student relationships. Most of my mentors and teachers do not even know that I exist, and that is the beauty of it all.

I am convinced that if people will heed this simple advice and find the right mentors for themselves, we will have more achievers, more innovations, more advancement, and more progress, and the world will be a much better place for it.

And now, without further ado, get to work immediately with securing yourself a great mentor.

Let's meet at the top!

Key Takeaways

- If you want accelerated progress and success in any area of your life: in relationships, career, business, finances, or spirituality, get yourself a suitable mentor.

- To have a mentor is to have "a brain to pick, an ear that listens, and a push in the right direction". To be mentored is to have someone who has travelled a particular road guide your every step and keep you out of 'potholes and land mines' that can derail or even devastate you.

- To be the best in the shortest possible time, you must learn from the best.

- Mentor-mentee relationships do not always have to be formal. Most of my mentors/teachers do not even know that I exist. Follow these steps to always gain access to the best minds:

  - **Step 1:** Pick a mentor/coach/teacher who shares a lot about their experience in books, blogs, videos, social media posts, etc.

  - **Step 2:** Read or watch everything they have ever created many times.

  - **Step 3:** Put what you have learnt from them into practice. You must apply what you learn. You must execute!

  - **Step 4:** Once you have applied what you learnt, consider teaching it to others as soon as possible. The more you teach, the more you achieve mastery of the subject. It is a universal principle.

CHAPTER 19

HOW AN ACCIDENTAL MENTORSHIP ENCOUNTER WITH A BILLIONAIRE CHANGED MY BUSINESS

"Great achievement is usually born of great sacrifice and is never the result of selfishness."
- Napoleon Hill

How and why does good fortune happen to some people but not others? I do not have the full answer, but I believe good fortune is more likely to happen when you are focused on SERVING others instead of focusing solely on your own needs.

I was once fortunate to say 'yes' to a request to serve and that experience was life transforming and destiny shaping. Here is the story of how I got accidentally mentored by a billionaire and how that experience became a game changer for my business.

A few months before my encounter, I was feeling stuck. I had hit a wall and was struggling to push ahead. It felt as if I had reached my limits, like I was on a treadmill and going nowhere fast. One morning, I was reading a book and I saw this sentence, "the best way to get unstuck is to focus on serving others". For some reason, it deeply resonated with me.

Up until then, I had been extremely self-focused and whining about how no one around me understood what I was going through and how all they wanted was to take and keep taking from me, how I was tired and how people were not pulling their weight and so on.

After reading that message, I decided to shift my thinking from myself to 'who' and 'how' I could help. Such a simple change in my philosophy has made such a significant difference in my business till date. The impact of this philosophy on my life and business has been so profound that over the years, I have had several reasons to apply it again and again to get me out of many troubles.

Not too long after my decision to change my philosophy, I received a call from a woman who was starting a new Non-Governmental Organization (NGO) and was looking for someone to facilitate their strategy sessions. A former client had referred her to me, and she indicated that she wanted me to help them out with the session. Shortly before we scheduled a face-to-face meeting to finalize our discussions, I wanted to find out if our working styles matched each other's, so I asked my typical diagnostic questions and I liked what I heard. Then, I asked her the final but critical question about their budget and if they could pay for my services. She laughed, saying that we would discuss the issue of budget and other logistics when we met. I had a funny feeling about her response but because she was clearly a fit with respect to the type of clients I liked to work with, I agreed to meet up with her the following week.

During our meeting, we discussed her aspirations at length and what she considered to be successful Strategy Retreat Session outcomes. I shared our approach to facilitating such a session, the time commitment expected from both parties, what must happen before, during and after the session, and other logistics. Then we got to the issue of our professional fees and that is where the problem started. I informed her of our rate and gave her a 10% discount because her organization was an NGO. She shocked me by pleading with me to accept an honorarium for the session. I asked her if she was kidding me, and she said she was not, launching into the typical pitch NGOs make when they want something for free or want to get you to work for little to nothing. I responded by giving her my well-rehearsed counter argument of how what she was asking for from us would not work and how she should consider getting a grant to pay for the project. I offered to appear as a guest speaker for an hour for free, but she wanted us to run the full 2 weeks pre-strategy activities, 3 days strategy sessions and 1-week post-strategy activities at 20% of our usual cost. I declined, of course. We went back and forth, ending the meeting without coming to a suitable agreement. I made a mental note to never have a meeting with her again, ever!

As expected, she expressed her disappointment, and said she would keep trying to get me to change my mind. That evening, she sent me a text. The same thing happened the next day. By the third day, when her text arrived, I was considering getting a restraining order when I saw the quote I had copied out about a month or two earlier on a post-it note near my bookshelf: ***When you are stuck, focus on*** *serving others*. At first, I rolled my eyes and pushed it out of my mind. However, the message kept nagging at me all day and by that evening, I had become restless. So, I gave her a call and said I would help her out, but that my decision to reconsider had nothing to do with her negotiation tactics.

Letting out a long laugh, she persuaded me to tell her what prompted a change of heart in me. For some strange reason, I decided to tell her the truth. I told her that I was experiencing a lull in my business, and that I was feeling stuck. Then I told her how I had come across the message to focus on serving others whenever one was stuck, that my acceptance to do the session was my attempt at following the philosophy. She was quiet for a while, finally commenting that what I had just told her was profound and that she would take it to heart and always remember it.

We planned the Strategy Retreat Project, and I went beyond the call of duty to execute it. Once I agree to do anything, I own it and do my best and then some.

At the end of the second day of the actual retreat workshop, my client told me that we would be having a guest speaker the next day. She mentioned that she had invited one of her mentors who she was also hoping would be willing to fund the NGO in the future and even become its chairman. I told her that it was fine, inquiring about her expectations and adjusting the third's day programme to accommodate the guest. Little did I know that I was about to have a mind-blowing experience.

When day three of the retreat came, the guest, a multi-billionaire and one of the top business executives in the country showed up. I was self-conscious and a bit nervous before my presentation, but by the end, it had gone very well, and he seemed genuinely impressed. He asked a lot of questions, most of which we had thoroughly addressed. As hoped, he committed right there on the spot to fund the organization. My client and her colleagues were over the moon. I was truly happy for them too. And I also wondered whether she would now be willing to pay our full rate. Afterall, the fortunes of her NGO had just changed, in part, due to my contributions.

Shortly afterwards, my client's guest invited me for dinner and said he would not take no for an answer. Of course, I was not prepared to decline his invitation, and gladly accepted it.

During the dinner, he mentioned that his mentee (my client) had told him everything about how she engaged my services including the reason why I agreed to take on her project. He then went on to share with me some of his philosophies about running his business. One of those philosophies completely changed my approach to business. Here is what he said to me that fateful evening: *Most business owners are short-distance runners in orientation. They want quick results, and they want it now. Unfortunately, great businesses are long distance races in nature and the misalignment between the orientation of business owners (or even career professionals) and the nature of great businesses (or careers) is the root cause of most failed or mediocre businesses or careers.*

Imagine trying to run a long-distance race with a short-distance mentality. It simply would not work. Such an individual is guaranteed to run out of steam, get stuck, burn out or eventually collapse or fail.

He carried on sharing that one of the best decisions a business owner or career professional could make was to adopt a *long-distance runner* mentality. He showed how he practiced this by first identifying a really big opportunity that he wanted to go after, an opportunity that if he succeeded in getting, would put him at a significant advantage (including financial freedom) for the next 10 to 15 years. Then he would count the cost and 'bury' his head for the next 3 years, if that is what it took to pursue and capture that opportunity. He shared examples of projects that he had worked on for 3 years non-stop, that had ended up taking care of his subsequent 15 to 20 years in business, thereby freeing him up to do whatever he wanted. He added that as soon as he discovered that the same efforts he put into harvesting big opportunities were commensurate to the efforts that smaller ones required, he asked himself, *why not always chase something big?* And that's what he began to do.

I later adopted his *long-distance runner* philosophy and termed it **Project 3:15.** Over the years I have developed several versions including **Project 2:10** (2 years to work on something big and 10 years to reap the rewards), **Project 5:20** (5 years to work on something massive and 20 years to reap the rewards), etc.

Something else he told me was that the adage, *good things come to those who wait,* was stupid. From his personal experience, good things came to those who worked hard for them and not those who waited. And the good news was that hard work did not require any special talent. Anybody can work hard. All that is required is a strong desire and wanting those good things badly enough. The question is, how badly do you want it?

After my dinner with him, I felt like I was floating on air. I could not believe my good fortunes. It was crystal clear to me that I had 'stumbled' upon a very important truth. The only issue was, would I only celebrate the wisdom I had just received and go on as if nothing had happened? God forbid! I could not sleep that night. I was determined to make sure I truly and fundamentally 'got' and internalized that message. I wrote it out on several post-it notes and placed them everywhere I could, in my bathroom, in my study, beside my bed, etc. I created an image of his message and made it my computer screen saver. This was not a message I ever wanted to forget.

Although I have since had the opportunity to learn from my new mentor several times after that first encounter, nothing ever came close to that first experience. The first cut is indeed the deepest.

I can attribute some of the major successes I have achieved to these two changes in philosophy: *Focus on serving others* and *adopt a long-distance runner mentality* in business. There have been times when I completely forgot them and started to lose momentum but going back to these fundamentals got me back on track.

I guarantee that if you adopt these two philosophies and consistently use them, you will achieve great things beyond your wildest imagination.

Key Takeaways

I believe that good fortune is more likely to happen to you when you are focused on SERVING others instead of on your own needs. When you are stuck, find someone to serve.

Most owners are short-distance runners in orientation. They want quick results, and they want it now. Unfortunately, building a great business requires a long-distance runner orientation. The misalignment between the short-term orientation of most business owners (and even career professionals) and the nature of great businesses (or careers) is the root cause of most failed or mediocre businesses or careers.

My mentor once told me that he attained financial freedom by practicing the long-distance runner philosophy. He did this by identifying a very big opportunity that he wanted to go after, an opportunity that if he succeeded in getting would put him at a significant advantage for the next 10-15 years. Then he counted the costs and 'buried his head' for the number of years that it took to pursue and capture that opportunity.

I adopted this long-distance runner approach. Over the years I have developed several versions including Project 2:10 (2 years to work on something big and 10 years to reap the rewards) and Project 5:20 (5 years to work on something massive and 20 years to reap the rewards).

I can attribute some of the major successes I have achieved to these two changes in my philosophy: Focus on serving others and adopting a long-distance runner mentality in business.

My mentor confirmed what I already know to be the truth: "Good things hardly ever come to those who wait idly." From experience, good things only come to those who work hard for them and not those who wait idly for them.

CHAPTER 20

BUILD YOUR PERSONAL ARMY OF ALLIES

"A person is a person through other persons."
- Archbishop Desmond Tutu

In his book *Never Eat Alone*, Keith Ferrazzi made a statement that has influenced my actions for many years. He said, "Poverty, I realized, wasn't only a lack of financial resources; it was isolation from the kind of people who could help you make more of yourself." How profound!

Conventional wisdom says that people who are very successful have three things in common. First, they have very high levels of motivation. Second, they are extremely capable people with strong abilities in their chosen fields. And third, they are masters at harnessing and maximizing their relationships.

Relationships mean absolutely everything in this world, everything. Nothing exists in isolation, not people, animals, or plants—nothing. Everything exists because it is in relationship with something else. This is even more true with people, and the longer I live, the more I realize that no one can succeed in this world if they are not skilled at relating with people. Our world is a world of people, and the business world is a world of businesspeople. To go far in anything, you will need the help of people. There is just no way around it. Nothing of great significance can be achieved alone. You will not achieve success without engaging the gifts, time, patronage, and abilities of others. Your greatness, significance, growth, development, and unique brand of achievement will depend on the support of your clients, colleagues, friends, protégés, subordinates, mentors, coaches, role models, parents, teachers, and many others. And so, to create a bright future for yourself you must have good people in your corner. You must have people who have the power to make a positive difference in your life and business rooting and cheering for you. Whatever your personality type, there is no escape, you must become a master at building your own personal army of allies.

In speaking of allies, I mean extremely valuable and powerful relationships. I am not referring to having countless phone numbers or many people's business cards. I am speaking of people with influence who like you and are willing to speak up for you in places you may never have access to. Allies are your strong base of supporters that know you and believe in you. They are not mere contacts; they are your strongest connections and your battle-ready companions, who are willing, able, and ready to go to war for you and to help you succeed.

Although these kinds of relationships are rare, they are possible and are crucial to your success. Your social capital, simply defined as the sum of the information, expertise, trust, and total value that exist in the relationships you have and social networks to which you belong, is your most valuable asset, next only to your health and vitality. Therefore, the commitment to building this kind of extremely rare but valuable resource is worth the energy and time that will be required. And the sooner you stop pretending that you can go alone and that you do not need people to succeed, the sooner you succeed.

Being good at what you do is great, but it will never be enough

Without the right social network to sell your competence to, of what importance is it? You and I know of several talented, highly skilled, and well-educated people who struggle to make any kind of headway in their careers or businesses simply because they lack the right network. I know this to be a fact because I was once one of those people and I deeply understand the pain and grief that comes from having first class abilities but subpar connections. This is very frustrating and heart breaking.

Therefore, when I give talks or coach people, I do my utmost to help them quickly realize that one of the coldest realities in the world is that there are certain heights that they will never ascend to on their own without the advantage of people to prop them up. In fact, it is no exaggeration to say that the breadth, length, height, and depth of your network determines the dimensions of your career or business. Your network and your career or business destiny are interwoven. Therefore, one of the most important business and life skills you will ever learn is how to find, court and win over the right people into your corner. And the best place to start is with the right mindset.

Dismantling wrong mindsets about networking

When the word networking is mentioned, what is your first unfiltered reaction? If it is a sense of dread about the awkwardness, the work required, and the uncertainties involved, you are in good company. I know many people who do not like to bother with this rather important aspect of their work life, and I really do not blame them. Networking has always been a stretch for me too, but the truth still remains that people are our most precious resource. So, it pays to change this mindset, by first developing an open-minded attitude towards networking. When a networking opportunity presents itself, be willing to say, *I don't know where this might lead, but I accept the unknown as a positive thing.* Understand that when we choose to do nothing about cultivating relationships, it will lead to nothing and nowhere. But when we choose to do something and continue to improve upon our relationship techniques, it will most likely lead to somewhere rewarding in the future.

Another unproductive mindset to drop is being too busy to network. Your active involvement with people is vital to increasing your probability of success. You cannot afford to be too busy to build relationships. If success is your aim, networking must become like breathing for you. You must embrace it as a natural way of life and do it every other day. Relationships that help you make the most of yourself hardly ever happen by chance. They must be proactively and very intensely pursued, courted, and nurtured if you are to succeed and keep out long term frustrations from your life.

A third mindset to change is that a person must be very extroverted to succeed in building relationships. If this is true, then it would mean that 56.8% [1] of the world's population will struggle to build solid networks. Thankfully, it is simply not true that only highly sociable people can succeed in building healthy networks. One way in which I solve this problem for myself is by choosing the networking approach and environment that play to my strengths.

In general, most introverted people shy away from networking because they think they will appear pushy. For others, the fear of rejection is too great. Marie McIntyre, author of *Secrets to Winning at Office Politics*, lists the following common complaints about networking and connecting with another person.

"I feel as though I'm bothering people."

"I don't know what to say."

"I hate talking to strangers."

"Most people don't have any job leads so it's a waste of time."

[1] According to a 2019 global research done by the Myers-Briggs company, 56.8% of the world's population prefer introversion.

"I hate saying the same thing over and over again."

"It's hard to sound upbeat when I'm totally depressed."

As McIntyre points out, behind these statements is the mistaken belief that every contact you make is one that will bring hiring opportunities or business deals. Approaching people with this mindset will only serve to hinder you. As a matter of fact, this mindset to 'get something from others' is what gives networking a bad name, it is simply not the right way to go about it.

Getting hired or getting business deals may be your ultimate goal, but if you leave that where it is—in the far distance—you will free yourself to take pleasure in the moment of meeting a new person and building a great professional relationship.

Let networking come as naturally as making new friends

When we set out to make friends, do we rush and crowd people's spaces or do we take it nice and easy and simply let the friendship take a natural course? I reckon that we tend to do the latter. The same should apply to building business relationships. Take it slow and steady. Enjoy the process and just be your best self.

I have never been someone that *hears* only; I have always made it a habit to *hear* and *do,* when what I hear is good and has the potential to change my life. And so, when I came across the relationship building wisdom that Dale Carnegie offered in his phenomenal book, *How to Make Friends and Influence People,* I took many of the relationship building tips very seriously and applied them till they produced results for me. And they sure did.

I am now going to share with you five relationship building principles that I learnt from Dale Carnegie and have since inculcated into my networking habits. Remember, these principles are not meant to enable you amass many phone numbers, business cards and LinkedIn connections; if that is your focus or habit, you will need to change it. Use these principles to start the process of deliberately courting those solid professional relationships that will become for you lifelong friends and allies.

Make the principles a lifestyle and you will find yourself never short of friendship opportunities, whether you are searching for friends or not. Bear in mind however, that when these principles open the door to a relationship, you will need to study and master the art of nurturing and nourishing relationships so that they continue to grow and intensify with time. The hardest part though is jumpstarting the professional relationship with someone you have identified as being strategic and valuable to your life, career, and business. And for this, these principles will help.

Five Ways to Spark off Relationship Building

According to the book of Proverbs, "a man who has friends must himself be friendly." Practice these five principles and you will find that they work wonders in building your relationships.

Principle One:
Become genuinely interested in other people

The fastest way to cheat yourself out of good relationships is to lack genuine interest in people. I read somewhere that the one who is not interested in his fellow men has the greatest difficulties in life. Don't be that person. Become truly interested in people and they will usually reciprocate. This is the best place to start your recruitment of allies. If you want to win over another person, first win their heart by showing genuine interest in them, and the rest of that person is likely to follow.

Principle Two:
Become a human magnet

The fastest way to do this is to go through life with a sincere smile for everyone you meet. This is a deeper way to live because a genuine smile can only come from a cheerful heart. And this means you must quickly deal with the negative energies and emotions that send out negative vibes and sours the face. The face has an unmanipulable way of betraying the heart, so you cannot fake a sincere smile for too long. If you do however work on your emotions and achieve the feat of always wearing a sincere smile that tells people that you like them, you will instantly become a magnet that draws people in effortlessly.

When you smile on the phone, it makes all the difference in your tone and makes you sound friendlier. In written communication, it is even more important to let your smile show through your expressions. Polite lines like: "I don't mean to trouble you…", "Would you be so kind as to…", "Thank you", "Please" and other courteous expressions show good manners that typically warms the hearts of people. So, have a smile on your face for everyone, whether you have intentions of friendship towards them or not. Amazing treasures sometimes spring up from the most unexpected sources when you spread your net far and wide. A cheerful disposition is a fantastic way to stay open to great relationships.

Principle Three:
Remember people's names

I recently read that when Southwest Airlines[2] took out a full-page newspaper advertisement to honor their late company founder, Herb Kelleher, the first line of the memorial text read, *"Dear Herb, thanks for always remembering our names."*

Remembering people's names is an advice that you have no doubt heard before. So, what exactly is in a name? *Why is it so important to remember people's names?* Understanding will come to you easily upon answering these two questions. One, when someone you have met only once and a long time ago remembers your name, doesn't it impress you and get your attention fast? Two, in a very noisy place, when someone says your name, doesn't the noise dim out immediately as you turn to the sweet sound that is your name? As it is with you, so it is with everyone else.

If you need any more proof as to why it is vital to recall people's names, here is more. A recent study using brain scans concluded that hearing your first name will activate parts of your brain different from those activated by hearing the names of other people. According to the scientists, "Adults never tire of hearing their names." If you embrace the power of recalling and using a person's name, you will be using a free, simple, and powerful tool in building stronger relationships with others.

Principle Four:
Always make people feel important and add value to others

The surest way to become special in another's eyes is to make them feel special. This is a law that the Lord Jesus summed up in one thought, "Do onto others as you would have others do unto you." If you invest good time and energy in devising ways to make your new contacts feel important, the chances for a stronger relationship will improve. Always remember that one of the deepest fundamental needs in human nature is the craving to be appreciated, whether we are royalty or regular people. We all want recognition of our true worth, and we all want to feel special. Anyone who can pull this off for us becomes a person we want to associate with.

If you want to make friends, go out of your way to do things for other people that make them feel special. Do sincere and heartfelt things that require your energy, time, and thoughtfulness. Believe me, people will recognize the effort, and will warm up to you. One writer takes this view, "I always say 'yes' to people and projects, wherever possible, wherever I know I can make a valuable contribution, whenever my priorities at home won't be compromised. The only theory behind this

[2] One of the major airlines of the United States and the world's largest low-cost carrier airline.

is that you never know where one thing, even the opportunity that looks small and unpromising, or the person who appears to already have everything they need for their business, may lead."

Principle Five:
Communicate to connect

At the start of a conversation with someone you want to build a relationship with, find common grounds. Focus your conversation on topics that also genuinely interest the other person. Emphasize your areas of similarities, not differences. Begin your conversations with things that you both agree on. If possible, search for what you both are passionate about and are striving for. In addition, encourage them to talk about themselves and truly listen with enjoyment. When they talk about things they love or enjoy, they will feel good and will associate those good feelings with you. That is a winning formula for making friends and influencing people.

The road to building a successful career or business could be daunting. Having decent, influential, and successful people who can make a difference in your life, career or business as allies makes the journey faster and easier. Believe me, whatever you invest in such good relationships is worth it.

That said, it is important to accept that some investments will not mature. Some people are only there to take what they can get from you and are closed to other possibilities. Such people are usually dead ends. Letting them dictate your response can deter your willingness to connect with others in the future. But if you are aiming for success, you will not allow them that measure of influence. You will be the kind of person who continues to see possibilities and potential around every corner.

Finally, always remember that life is very much like a game of chess. Only those who have mastered the rules and strategies play it best and succeed. One of the greatest rules of business is: *Who you know determines where you end up, either on high grounds or valleys low.*

Key Takeaways

- Nothing of great significance can be achieved alone. If you will create a bright future for yourself, you must have good people in your corner, people who have the power to make a difference in your life and business rooting and cheering for you. You must become a master at building your own personal army of allies.

- When I say allies, I am speaking of extremely valuable and powerful relationships, not a legion of numbers in your phonebook or of people's business cards. I speak of people with influence that like you and are willing to speak for you in places you may never reach. Allies are your strong base of supporters that know you and believe in you. They are not mere contacts, but your strongest connections and battle-ready companions. They are those who are willing, able, and ready to go to war for you and help you succeed.

- These kinds of relationships are rare, but possible, and are crucial to your success. You and I know several talented, highly skilled, and well-educated people who struggle to make any kind of headway in their careers or businesses simply because they lack the right network.

- Treat networking as naturally as making new friends. I benefitted greatly from five powerful relationship building principles that I learnt from Dale Carnegie because I infused them into my networking habits. You should do the same. The five principles for sparking off relationships are:

  - Become genuinely interested in other people.

  - Be a human magnet.

  - Remember people's names.

  - Always make people feel important and add value to others.

  - Communicate to connect.

- That said, it is important to accept that some investments will not yield returns. Some people take what they can get from you and are closed to other possibilities. Such people are usually dead ends. Aiming for mediocrity means you will let such people dictate your response and deter your willingness to connect with others in the future, but if you are aiming for success, you will not allow this to happen.

- Take the pains to network because one of the greatest rules of business is: *Who you know determines where you end up, either on the high grounds or the valleys low.*

CHAPTER 21

THE PARADOXES OF LIFE THAT DETERMINE SUCCESS

*"Seek freedom and become captive of your desires.
Seek discipline and find your liberty."*
- Frank Herbert

Millions of people live darkened and deeply frustrated lives because the paths to success in life are mainly counterintuitive. Indeed, if attaining success were easy, the world would be brimming over with successful people. If the path to success was instinctive there would be no need for elaborate principles of success. But, no, the world is full of paradoxes, and one of the most interesting things I have discovered is this: *the factors that create success are not natural to the way we are wired to think and behave*, and this poses a very huge challenge.

For instance, to hit a golf ball farther, you need to hold the club more loosely. To stabilize a car on a very slippery road, you should take your foot off the brake. To strengthen a plant and make it grow faster, you must trim it back.

Business is also rife with paradoxes. If a business is in trouble, it must shrink to grow. It must focus its resources on its biggest opportunities. From focused efforts comes growth and by narrowing scope, one creates expansion.

Back to the subject of how we live our lives. I have repeatedly found that most things that create success and happiness in life are counterintuitive. Except we choose to live consciously and engage with life intentionally, we can easily end up living a mediocre life full of pointless difficulties, avoidable obstacles, needless frictions, and unnecessary problems. We must avoid living by default because that mode of living can be devastating to our very existence.

The more I meditate on it, the clearer it becomes to me that the very areas where we naturally tend to be intuitive in our approach to life are the very ones where we must become intentional if we will unlock our huge potential, take massive action, and achieve colossal success.

Consider this with me. It is instinctive for us as human beings to focus on our own needs and what we can get out of a situation. It is counterintuitive to focus on serving others and meeting their needs. In the end, which one of these two paths would you say has the potential to create wealth and happiness? Focusing on serving others, you will no doubt agree.

It is impulsive to focus on your weaknesses and keep trying to improve them whilst ignoring your strengths. It is an intentional act to focus on leveraging your strengths for maximum advantage. In the long run, which one of these two choices promises to have the greatest impact on your growth? Making the most of your strengths does so, and by many miles.

It is impulsive to attempt to do a lot of things well. It is counterintuitive to focus on doing one thing exceptionally well, better than anyone else in the world. At the end of the day, which of the two would have the potential to make you great? Of course, doing one thing exceptionally well. By the way, no one can do everything exceptionally well. So, it becomes vital to ask yourself, what is my one thing that if done exceptionally well can be the difference that makes a massive difference? Find it. And give it everything you have got till you become exceptional at it.

It is instinctive to allow things that go wrong—our mistakes, losses, etc., to upset us, weigh us down and destabilize us completely. It is counterintuitive to realize that whenever things go wrong, there are lessons and opportunities for us inherent in them.

It is impulsive to be afraid of failing, and therefore decide not to take risks or try out new things. It is very counterintuitive to risk failure in a bid to attempt and achieve great things.

It is instinctive to try to grab hold of every opportunity that comes your way. It takes a strong act of the will to avoid getting distracted by shiny objects and focus disproportionately on your core objectives.

It is impulsive to multitask and try to do several things at once. It is more intentional and productive to focus on one thing and bring it to completion, before moving on to the next and then the one after.

It is in the human nature to get easily bored with an area where one is winning or succeeding in and abandon it in search of shiny new objects. It is a mark of deep business wisdom to double down your efforts on what is working and make the most of that victory. I have learnt the hard way that when one is winning, the best growth strategy to adopt is to dig deeper, mine further and make the most of that identified 'goldmine', rather than abandoning it out of boredom or in pursuit of the latest new thing.

It is impulsive to spend all the resources that you have right now. It takes discipline to reinvest and allow compound interest to do its magic.

It is impulsive to meet someone new and talk endlessly about yourself and your accomplishments. It is savvier to listen and let the other person feel heard and important.

It is instinctive for entrepreneurs to fall madly in love with their products and services, to the extent that they get stuck in a rut. It is however more strategic to create a product and then emotionally detach from it, put it out there, observe it and measure how the product performs, judging it on its own merit and letting the marketplace decide whether it is a winner.

It is impulsive to keep working on an idea or product until it is perfect before launching it in the marketplace. However, the wisdom gained from many lost battles demands that one launches an imperfect product, get feedback, improve, and then relaunch. Like the saying goes, DONE will always be better than NONE.

It is very instinctive to go to great lengths to shield our kids and protect them from failing or making mistakes. It is however in their best interests that we let them fail and make their own mistakes and learn from it. Otherwise, they can never grow and realize their full potential.

It is human nature to do everything possible to avoid pressure and stress and to look for short-cuts or take the easy roads. It takes a lot of wisdom to recognize that consistently putting ourselves under high pressure and stretch situations is the only route to personal growth and self-development. It is simply impossible to advance without putting ourselves in situations that stretch us.

It is impulsive to think short-term, right here and now, and to seek instant gratification. It is very intentional to think long-term and delay gratification, but it is also the only way to amount to anything worthy of admiration.

It is instinctive to try to please others. It is completely counterintuitive to realize the futility of living your life to please everyone. The most guaranteed way to fail in life is to live your life trying to please other people.

So, folks, there you have it. I can go on and on, but I am sure by now, that you get my drift.

If you want to be happy and successful in life, become very aware of those intentional things that you must do to make it happen. Do not get trapped in life by allowing your mind run perpetually in an 'impulsive mode', by allowing yourself to do only those things that automatically feel easy. You need to be deliberate about doing the hard but right and very intentional things that will ensure that your future is full of comfort and happiness. It is critical that you constantly check that you are not allowing your default self to run your life.

Live intentionally. Live consciously. Live strategically.

Key Takeaways

- Life and business are rife with paradoxes. The factors that create success and happiness are not natural to the way we are wired to think and behave, and this poses a very huge challenge.

- To be happy and successful in life, be very aware of those intentional things that you must do to make it happen. Don't get trapped in life by allowing your mind run perpetually on an 'impulsive mode'; and by allowing yourself to do only those things that automatically feel easy.

- To make significant progress in life, be deliberate about doing the hard but right things that will ensure that your future is full of comfort and happiness.

CHAPTER 22

FOLLOW THE SUCCESS MAPS; AVOID THE FAILURE TRAPS

"The greatest danger in business and life lies not in outright failure but in achieving success without understanding why you were successful in the first place."

- Robert Burgelman

In the world of music and record labels, one of the biggest fears of rising singers is the ever-looming possibility of being a one-hit wonder, the fear of not being able to reproduce or exceed their previous successes. The same is true in the world of business leaders, executives, and career professionals. Every new financial year or quarter marks the dawn of a fresh start, a new target, and a new challenge. The previous wins are all but forgotten and every eye is fixed on the new ball. This is a tough way to live without a dependable plan to replicate your wins.

The truth is that the world of business is tough and cold-hearted, and the possibility of failure is always around the corner. *It is one thing to get to the top and it is a very different thing to stay there.* Therefore, the challenge that confronts every business leader and career professional in today's volatile world is not how to win once, but how to keep winning.

I once read a story about a young man who became a multi-millionaire after he developed an exciting mobile application that was eventually sold for 750 million dollars to a Fortune 500 company. For the sake of this book, we will call him Jack. A few months after selling off his mobile application, Jack decided to enroll in an Ivy League University to study an MBA. When one of the professors responsible for the admission process saw his application, he was surprised but curious to know why the young man decided to enroll for the MBA.

During the pre-admission interview, the professor said to Jack, "I have gone through your application, and I am intrigued. By every standard, you are already very financially successful. Why do you consider it necessary to register for an MBA? What's your objective for taking this MBA programme when you are already so successful?"

Jack's response was simple. "Yes, I agree that I have attained some financial success. However, the challenge is that I don't really understand why I was successful in the first place. I am afraid that if I don't deeply understand how I came to be so successful the first time, I might not be able to replicate or sustain that success. So, I reckoned that an MBA programme would show me exactly what I did to create the success I have achieved, so that I may codify it, replicate it and sustain my success in the future."

Jack was wise. If you do not understand the basics of how you achieved the success you have or the progress you have made, your chances of replicating that success or progress are very slim. And this applies whether you are a career professional or business owner. The dynamic processes of success can be subtle but extremely powerful, and a failure to *recognize* and *replicate* them can mean the difference between struggling and succeeding. Some of my struggles in business have arisen from violating this principle. So, do you really know how to duplicate your success? Begin finding out today by answering these questions.

What is your proven strategy for navigating the increasingly complex, volatile, and uncertain business climate?

What is your tried and trusted plan that guarantees that you will keep winning?

What is your protocol for navigating your way out of difficult corners and forging ahead?

Most people I have met are unable to come up with coherent answers to these vital questions, and not so long ago, I was one of such people. When my mentor posed these questions to me several years ago, I found myself floundering and unable to give clear answers, which came as a surprise to me because I had always taken pride in my strategic thinking ability.

Upon noticing my troubled countenance, my mentor tried to assure me that being unable to answer these questions with clarity was quite understandable. Afterall, not many people took the time to consider such questions, let alone have clear answers to them. That response did little to buoy me up because it did not eliminate the fact that without a business contingency protocol, I was literally standing on sinking sand. I did not need anyone to tell me that doing business in a volatile, uncertain, complex, and ambiguous environment without a proven plan to manage the inevitable storms was a bad idea.

We got to work immediately, and the first thing my mentor showed me was that to answer the questions with clarity, I needed to ask myself even more powerful questions such as:

- How have I made progress or gotten ahead in the past?

- How have I gotten unstuck or beaten the odds successfully in the past?

- Where have I succeeded in the past and how did I achieve that success? What was the plan or pattern that created that progress or success?

- Is it replicable and predictable?

- What is in my DNA? What is it that I am really good at?

Thinking through and answering these questions with clarity turned out to be one of the most important activities I have ever done, because in thoroughly answering them, I found two things to be true. First, that success is predictable. Second, Jim Collins was right when he said, "The undisciplined pursuit of more is how the mighty fall."

The Predictability of Success

Behavioral scientists have discovered that areas of past successes predict areas of future successes, and areas of past performance predicts areas of future performance, meaning that you are more likely to be successful in the future where you have succeeded in the past. Of course, this in no way implies that you cannot change and succeed in a completely different arena. What it really means is that the building blocks for your future success, the foundations required, will most likely be the same building blocks from your previous successes.

In corroborating this, Robert Burgelman, a Business Strategy Professor at Stanford Graduate School, aptly noted that "One of the biggest, and most strategic mistakes lies in failing to aggressively and persistently make the most of victories." If we drill down to the basics, we will find that there are two fundamental causes of the one-hit wonder phenomenon. The first cause is a failure to deeply understand the underlying factors that gave rise to the progress in the first place. The second cause is a failure to replicate successful patterns again and again. Success is not that complicated.

So, in what area(s) have you succeeded in the past? Did you maximize it, or did you abandon it in search of the newest trends and latest fads? Did you trade it for so-called greener pastures? Doing so almost always turns out to be a big mistake.

It is widely known that 9 out of 10 new initiatives fail. Why? Simply because they are new, unknown, and unproven, and as a result, it takes a lot of time to build them up to speed, and a lot of resources to stabilize them. If resources are infinite and you have a lot of time on your hands, then, feel free to speculate and experiment with as many new initiatives as you like. But if resources are scarce and the time to experiment is extremely limited, you will need to get very good at uncovering your hidden successes and assets. These are things that you already possess or have acquired over time whose value, properties, or potentials you have not fully appreciated, realized, or leveraged.

Therefore, taking the time to understudy your success patterns is vital to multiplying and reproducing that success in future. Over the years, I have become very good at identifying and maximizing my hidden assets and helping others to do the same. Without fail, I have repeatedly observed that whenever people take the time to uncover and properly deploy their hidden assets, they move from a position of struggle to a position of success. It may sound too simple to be true, but it is true. However, the reason why many people are unable to tap into this resource is because they are way too close to the issue to self-diagnose and uncover their own hidden assets. In such cases, coaches and mentors are simply invaluable.

And if you are thinking to yourself that you do not have any past success that you can leverage as a foundation to build your future successes, (even though I seriously doubt that could ever be the case), there is a solution for that: *Learn from other people's successes!*

The Trap of More, More, More

In addition to understudying and duplicating your previous successes, one trap to avoid and steer clear of, if you will beat the odds and achieve success, is the trap of not regulating your desire to do more and more new things. I have witnessed first-hand that companies and individuals do not fail because of doing too little they fail from doing too much. This phenomenon has been referred to as the *undisciplined pursuit of more.*

I know this because I used to serve as both the CEO and Chairman of the 'undisciplined pursuit of more' committee. I simply cannot count the number of times I have stretched myself and my resources too thin to the extent that they became ineffectual, leading to outright failure or mediocre results at best.

By every measure, this has been one of the greatest struggles I have had to contend with in business. Even though I am intelligent enough to know that the undisciplined pursuit of more is a guarantee for failure, I have repeatedly managed to convince myself that I did not have any other choice. I even have a Bible passage to justify this unhealthy behavior. "Cast thy bread upon the waters: for thou shalt find it after many days. Give a portion to seven, and also to eight; for thou knowest not what evil shall be upon the earth".[3]

It took a while and extensive discussions with a couple of my mentors for me to finally understand that the root cause of my tendency to do way too much for my own good arose from *extreme survival mentality.* Out of my desperation to survive, my instincts urge me to hedge my bets by doing so much so that if one, two, three or even four ventures fail, then I have a fifth that I can count on to be the winner. This mentality has cost me more than I could have imagined.

How I Beat the Odds and Multiply my Wins

So, what have I learned from my successes and failures? What has become my plan for getting ahead, staying unstuck, beating the odds, and achieving success in today's extremely volatile world?

After years of searching, with millions of naira invested, and thousands of hours of sweat and tears, I have found that my go-to formula for getting unstuck and making progress no matter the situation I find myself in, is a simple 4-step process:

Step 1: Take ownership.

Step 2: Focus on serving others.

Step 3: Be a student (revisit past success patterns and understudy others' successes).

Step 4: Execute.

Step 5: Rinse and repeat.

I do not insist on being right. All I ask is that you think about what I am sharing with you, really think about it and decide for yourself, if and how you can apply them to your context.

As a business owner, you do not have a revenue or growth problem, nor an economic

[3] Ecclesiastes 11:1-2

crisis problem, what you have is an unwillingness to focus on solving the problems of others. What you have is an 'unwillingness to be a student' problem.

As an individual, you do not have a lack of employment problem. You do not have a low earning income potential problem. You have an unwillingness to focus on solving others' problems. You are unwilling to be a student.

Key Takeaways

- It is one thing to get to the top and a very different thing to stay there. The challenge that confronts every business leader and professional in today's volatile world is not how to win once, but how to keep winning.

- If you don't understand the basics of how you achieved the success that you have or the progress you have made, your chances of replicating that success or progress are very slim. And this applies whether you are a career professional or business owner. The dynamics of success can be subtle but extremely powerful, and a failure to recognize and replicate them can mean the difference between struggling and succeeding.

- *What is your proven strategy for navigating the increasingly complex, volatile, and uncertain business climate? What is your tried and trusted plan that guarantees that you keep on winning? What is your protocol for finding your way out of difficult corners and forging ahead?*

- To answer these questions with clarity, ask yourself more powerful questions about your past like:

  - How have I made progress or gotten ahead in the past?
  - How have I gotten unstuck or beaten the odds successfully in the past?
  - Where have I succeeded in the past and how did I achieve that success? What was the plan or pattern that created the progress or success?
  - Is it replicable and predictable?
  - What is in my DNA? What is it that I am really good at?

- Success is predictable. "One of the biggest, and most strategic mistakes lies in failing to aggressively and persistently make the most of victories". Jim Collins was right when he said, "The undisciplined pursuit of more is how the mighty fall."

- To beat the odds and multiply your wins:

  - Take ownership.

- Focus on serving others.
- Be a student (revisit past success patterns and understudy others' successes).
- Execute.
- Rinse and repeat.

CHAPTER 23

WHY PRAYING AGAINST YOUR ENEMY MIGHT ACTUALLY BE A VERY BAD IDEA

"When there is no enemy within, the enemies outside cannot hurt you."
- African Proverb

I do not know about you, but I have come to a very carefully considered conclusion and I am absolutely convinced of the fact that I, Bolaji Olagunju, am without a shadow of doubt my own worst enemy. And that is why you can never find me praying against my enemy. Never! I have come face to face with my worst enemy and it is me.

If you are wondering what exactly I mean by 'praying against one's enemies', it is a method of prayer that many of us in developing West African countries, especially in Nigeria, employ. The aim of this prayer is to eliminate any and every obstacle that stands in the way of our progress.[4]

In any case, it turns out that often, when it comes to making progress in life, whether personally or professionally, a lot depends on us as individuals. The factors that make for success are more internally motivated as opposed to being externally driven. Before I say anymore, let us examine the definition of the word 'enemy'.

Who is an enemy? According to Oxford Languages Dictionary, "An enemy is a person who is actively opposed or hostile to someone or something." If we appropriate this definition to our context, we can correctly define our enemy as anyone who is actively opposed or hostile to our personal or professional progress. Think about this definition deeply for a few seconds. It has scary implications because when we objectively and honestly zoom in on the reasons for our lack of progress, we often find that the real enemy is none other than our self-sabotaging thoughts and behavior

[4] The idea of praying against one's enemies may have been borrowed from the Psalms of King David of Israel in the Old Testament or inherited from traditional African religions.

that are hostile to success.

Those repetitive, self-defeating behaviors such as procrastination, paralysis by analysis, perfectionism, over complication of simple things, doing too much and spreading oneself too thin, taking things too personally, untamed fear of rejection, overly defensive behavior, not learning from one's mistakes, inadequate preparation, choosing to walk away when things are difficult and so on, are the behind-the-scene culprits that hold us back from achieving the kind of success that we so desire. And for as long as we continue to indulge these behaviors, we will always be our own enemy.

As a case in point, let us talk about our old and most popular enemy, procrastination, that dreadful urge most of us suffer from, when we know there is work to be done, and yet we put it off for as long as possible, sometimes till the very last minute. How many times has procrastination robbed you of the small wins that could have led to the big win? How many times has paralysis by analysis kept you from executing your brilliantly written business plans? How many times have you set your own deadlines for a project and for some unknown reason, failed to meet it? How many times have you let temporary setbacks bind your hands and feet from trying again?

The major sign that an organization suffers from chronic corporate self-defeating behaviors is that goals are repeatedly set but **not** met. Eventually, this continuous cycle of *unachieved goals* and *unmet targets* leads to loss of productivity, results, and growth, and this is the number one reason most businesses die and many careers grind to a standstill. Self-defeating behaviors are always the enemies and not some unknown person somewhere else.

While addressing a University of Washington audience about how he and Bill Gates became so successful, Warren Buffet said, "Everybody here has the ability to do anything I do and much beyond. Some of you will, and some of you won't. For those who won't, it will be because you **get in your own way,** not because the world doesn't allow you to."

Love or hate him, you cannot deny the wisdom in this quote by Bishop David Oyedepo: "There is no mountain anywhere; every man's ignorance is his mountain." Every man's self-sabotaging behavior is his own mountain, and this is so true for me and for a lot of people I know.

Personally, one of my biggest self-sabotaging behaviors, and probably one of yours too, is the failure to do what I know is good, and even critical for me. I have often wondered about this, and I eventually discovered the reason.

Several years ago, I was fortunate to attend a Leadership Development Programme at Harvard University, and one of the most fascinating sessions was with Professor Kevin Kegan. Professor Kegan has spent a lifetime studying the phenomenon of why people do not do what they are supposed to do, and he captured his findings in a very fascinating book titled *Immunity to Change.* In the book, he shared a very interesting, but disturbing finding about a medical study that showed that even after heart doctors told their seriously at-risk heart patients that they would literally die if they did not make dietary changes to their personal lives, do more exercises, and quit smoking, only one in seven patients made those changes. One in seven! It was not a case of whether they lacked a sense of urgency or motivation. What could be more urgent or motivating than a chance to avoid early death by making lifestyle changes? Even though the doctors made sure they knew just what they needed to do and what would happen if they did not do it, six out of seven patients still ignored it!

According to Professor Kegan, this finding, among others, confirms an age-long suspicion that human beings indeed seem to have an extremely active resistance to change. In his words, "We uncovered a phenomenon we call 'the immunity to change,' a heretofore hidden dynamic that actively (and brilliantly) prevents us from changing because of its devotion to preserving our existing way of making meaning." This in turn corroborates what I have found to be true, that most people or businesses do not have a knowledge problem, they have a failure to execute what *they already know* problem. This lack of discipline to do what we need to do, when we need to do it, whether we feel like it or not, is the core reason why many people struggle through life.

Therefore, I never pray for my enemies to hug a faulty transformer when it is raining heavily because I might just be praying against myself. And I genuinely think you should stop doing so too if that is your sole strategy for making your desired progress. For all you know, your continued struggle might just be because you are actually 'praying against' yourself!

However, if you must absolutely pray against your enemy, do try to qualify who the other enemy is so that your prayers might be appropriately targeted. Praying against an undefined enemy might be bad for you in the long run because if you are like me, with what I know about myself, prayers targeted at your enemies could be prayers aimed at yourself. My advice is, just stop it! First, be sure that you have put your house in order, and that you have stopped being an obstacle in your own path. Do this first before yielding to the temptation on easy street to pray against an 'unknown enemy'.

Key Takeaways

- Making progress in our personal or professional life depends a lot on us as individuals. The factors that make for success are more internally motivated as opposed to being externally driven.

- Often, the real enemy of our progress is none other than our self-sabotaging thoughts and behavior that oppose success. The repetitive, self-defeating behaviors are procrastination, paralysis by analysis, perfectionism, over complication of simple things, doing too much and spreading oneself too thin, taking things too personally, untamed fear of rejection, overly defensive behavior, not learning from one's mistakes, not preparing adequately enough or choosing to walk away when things are difficult etc. They are the behind-the-scenes culprits that hold us back from achieving the kind of success that we desire. And for as long as we continue to indulge them, we will always be our own enemy.

- The major sign that an organization suffers from chronic corporate self-defeating behaviors is that goals are repeatedly set but not met. Eventually, this continuous cycle of unachieved goals and unmet targets leads to loss of productivity, results, and growth, and this is the number one reason why most businesses die and many careers grind to a halt. These behaviors are always the enemy and not some unknown person somewhere.

- *"There is no mountain anywhere; every man's ignorance is his mountain."* Every man's self-sabotaging behavior is his own mountain. Everybody can be successful if they will but get out of their own way.

- Research has found that human beings seem to have an extremely active resistance to change. This in turn corroborates what I have found to be true, that most people or businesses do not have a knowledge problem, they have a failure to execute what they already know problem.

- Stop praying against your so-called enemies of progress. You might be praying against yourself. Be sure that you have put your house in order, and you have stopped being an obstacle in your own path. Do this first before yielding to the temptation to pray against an 'unknown enemy'. For all you know, your continued struggle might be the result of you actually 'praying against' yourself!

CHAPTER 24

YOUR RENEWAL IS CRITICAL TO VICTORY

"There's nothing more important than our good health – that's our principal capital asset."
- Arlen Specter

The winner of the Indianapolis 500-mile race, an annual American automobile race and a major global motorsport event, is usually not the one who drives the fastest, the longest, and most continuously. The winner is the one who makes the most efficient pit stops along the way to refuel, change their tires, and make mechanical adjustments and repairs. Why? Renewal is as important to victory as the race itself.

As this is true for cars, it is even truer for humans. Our makeup is more complex, with more moving body parts than most machines. Yet, most of us take better care of our cars than we do our bodies. We disregard and push our bodies hard because of our jobs, eating junk food with little to no exercise, and inadequate sleep, thinking we are using our strengths to our advantage. Unfortunately, it is the other way round; we are gradually depleting our fundamental stores of energy, and for most of us, these stores are non-renewable. Strength overused or abused eventually becomes a liability. Working hard without taking quality time to rest and exercise leads to the very thing we are working hard to beat—ineffectiveness and poor performance—because of the accompanying stress, anxiety, and sickness. And if a person pushes his luck so hard till that luck runs out, shocking and untimely death can be the result.

In the early years of my entrepreneurial journey, I thought success required working unforgiving hours. I was always working, constantly building, growing, and skipping my necessary periods of rest and renewal. As the years and the stress took its toll, I learned the hard way that *being busy* and *being successful* were not the same thing.

It is not the number of hours you work that really matters, rather it is how much value you create in what you do. It is the quantity and quality of energy you bring into whatever hours you work that determine the value that will be generated. Therefore, the most important factor to creating a quality life is energy—how you spend and renew it. Resist the temptation to think that the best way to get more done is to continuously work longer hours. This always proves to be the ultimate self-sabotage and a path that is destined to produce exhaustion rather than success. As important as it is to work, it is equally important to have a plan for rest, relaxation, self-care, and quality sleep.

Rest is not a luxury; it is a necessity

Today's world tends to vilify periods of rest. Periods for breaks and vacation are viewed as luxuries and privileges. This is a destructive idea and one that I believe is responsible for the increase in chronic diseases and a lower life expectancy globally. We tend to treat being stressed and overworked as a badge of honor, an indicator of commitment to one's work. Many people have paid for this error of judgement with their lives. Rest is not a luxury, and the kind of break from work that is necessary for renewal is the kind that sociologists call detachment, the ability to put work completely out of your mind and attend to other things for a period. This temporary detachment from work is tremendously important as a source of mental and physical recovery from work. It is critical if you will continue to do your very best work and prevent burnout that can lead to emotional exhaustion, a decline in performance, poorer decision-making, lower empathy, and higher rates of errors.

Whether we like it or not, the body eventually retaliates when we abuse it by working long hours with little or no time for renewal and rejuvenation. Human beings are not meant to run like computers—at high speeds, continuously, and for long periods of time. The more hours you work and the longer you go without real renewal, the more you begin to default reflexively into behaviors such as impatience, frustration, distraction, and disengagement, that reduce your own effectiveness. And these are the less tragic side effects of a lack of rest and renewal. In a nine-year study of twelve thousand men at high risk for coronary heart disease, researchers found that those who took annual vacations had fewer heart attacks and lower overall mortality rates than men who did not.

One writer wisely said that our bodies are our machines for living. They are organized for that as it is their nature. Science has proven that every single cell in the human body replaces itself over a period of seven years. Thus, if we enable our bodies by healthy living with optimal periods of breaks, we will free up the lifecycle within us to go on unhindered and our bodies will be better able to defend itself. In this way, the body will do more for us than if we cripple it by weighing it down with all sorts of synthetic remedies after weakening it with stress and delayed renewal.

Therefore, whatever you do, no matter the type of schedule you run or whatever weight of responsibility you bear, create time to rest and renew yourself. Make it a habit to take care of your body. It is literally the only 'irreplaceable house' you must live in. And do not wait any longer to begin to live and rest right, be deliberate about it. Work it into your schedule like you schedule your business meetings. Treat your periods of rest as sacred. To delay in doing this always proves to be a costly mistake. Time is ticking away. If you have never made diet, rest, and exercise a priority, do not wait until the fuse is blown because you do not have an unlimited supply of replacements. Most deaths in middle age occur because of protracted habits of neglecting one's health. Work hard but be smart about it. Your effectiveness, your results, your success, your wellbeing, your life—all of you—depends on it.

Key Takeaways

- Working hard without making out quality time to rest and renew yourself leads to the very thing we are working hard to beat—ineffectiveness and poor performance from stress, anxiety, and sickness. And if a person pushes his luck so hard that luck runs out, untimely death can result.

- In a nine-year study of twelve thousand men at high risk for coronary heart disease, researchers found that those who took annual vacations had fewer heart attacks and lower overall mortality rates than men who did not.

- Whether we like it or not, the body retaliates against the abuse of working long hours with little or no time for renewal and rejuvenation. Human beings are not meant to run like computers—at high speeds, continuously, for long periods of time.

- Busy and successful are not the same thing. It is not the number of hours you work that really matters; it is how much value you create by what you do. It is the quantity and quality of energy you bring into whatever hours you work that determine the value that will be generated. Therefore, the most important factor to creating a quality life is how you spend and renew your energy.

- Periods for breaks and vacation are erroneously viewed as luxuries and privileges. Resist the temptation to think that the best way to get more done is to continuously work longer hours. This always proves to be the ultimate self-sabotage and a path that produces exhaustion rather than success. As important as it is to work, it is equally important to have a plan for rest, relaxation, self-care, and quality sleep.

- Most deaths in middle age occur because of protracted habits of health neglect. Work hard but be smart about it. Your effectiveness, results, success, wellbeing, and life—all of you, is at stake.

CHAPTER 25

BEWARE OF THE DISCOURAGEMENT COMMITTEE

"The person who says it cannot be done should not interrupt the person who is doing it."
- Chinese Proverb

I consider it critically important to dismantle a destructive, yet widely prevalent and limiting idea, that *you need the validation of others to pursue your dreams.*

I became compelled to free people from the shackles of this belief by sharing my personal story, when for the fourth time in less than three months, I had to spend a significant amount of time encouraging someone who had been told by their so-called mentor— someone that they actually looked up to— that they were not allowed to punch above their weight, that they had to wait for their time and not run ahead of the people in front of them. What utter rubbish! What a load of baloney!

If you have ever experienced this sort of thing at any point in your journey to making life better for yourself, this chapter is dedicated to you. If you have been told what you can or cannot do by those that position themselves as 'elders' and 'experts' in any field—I call them the *Discouragement Committee*, if people have set up roadblocks and created obstacles to prevent you from making progress and getting ahead; if someone somewhere is trying to put a lid on your God-given potential, you must do whatever it takes to keep them from holding you down. And I assure you that the story I am about to share with you will be game-changing for you and your future.

When I first entered the HR Consulting business, I was both ignorant and naive, with absolutely no idea of the painful and brutal realities that awaited me. I went into business with the assumption that I would be able to count on people who were my closest associates for consulting briefs. This assumption proved so devastatingly inaccurate that it almost caused me to fail and leave the business.

Contrary to what I expected, a large percentage of those closest to me appeared to be the ones desperately wanting me to fail. I am talking about close friends who were actively blocking opportunities that were available to everyone else. Their actions baffled me in no small measure. Why would a friend be unwilling to give me a fair chance to demonstrate what I could do? And no, I was not looking for handouts, absolutely not! I just wanted the same level playing field afforded to others in my field. I quickly realized that I had better chances of getting a shot from complete strangers than people I knew.

The experience I am about to relate taught me my first business lesson, one that has helped me over the years: *When it comes to success in business, most times, you stand a better chance of getting a much-needed break from strangers.*

This encounter stood out for me as the most painful because it happened at the very difficult start-up phase of my business. A friend who was also the head of Human Resources of a large organization invited me for a meeting at his office. Thinking that I had finally gotten a chance to showcase what my business could do, I prepared and printed a full colored presentation, spending the money I really could not afford for this apparent business opportunity. On getting to my friend's office, it turned out that all he wanted to see me for was to find out how my new business was doing and how I was coping with paying salaries and managing the home front.

Again, I thought that if he knew how bad things were, perhaps, he would at least stop blocking me and give me the opportunity to pitch for recruitment, training, or outsourcing briefs that my business did so well. I launched into the story of how dire my financial circumstances were, how I had to refinance my car to pay salaries and school fees, and how if something did not change in the next 2-3 months, I would be back in the job market. But all my stories fell on disinterested ears. He did not change his stand towards me.

After my experience that day, I learnt perhaps the second most valuable lesson I learnt in business — *Never ever let people you need something from get the impression that your back is against the wall, and that you are fast running or have completely run out of options.*

Till this day (by the way, that incident happened in 2004), the look on my friend's face and his reaction to my tale of woe is as vivid to me as if it happened yesterday. He leapt to his feet, saying to my face, "See your life? Do you think that people like me who have decided not to set up our own consulting firms do not know what we are doing? Do you think it is that easy? Well, you have yourself to blame. Mister, you better update your CV and start looking for a job before it is too late. I can even help you speak to a couple of people who might be able to help you get a job."

To say that I was stunned is to put it mildly. The obvious relief on his face when he heard my business was not doing well at that point, and the gleeful manner with which he said what he said haunted me for days. But it was also a turning point for me, as it marked the beginning of learning how things really worked in the world of business.

That incident is one of many such encounters that I experienced in the early part of my start-up journey.

If you ever find yourself in a situation where you talk to established people in your area of interest about starting out or advancing your career in that area, and they go to great lengths to tell you how challenging the profession is, how it is almost impossible for a newcomer to get started, how many years of experience and the number of qualifications a person must have to succeed in that field, and why it would be a mistake for you to enter their field, thank them for their time but please take their 'advice' with a pinch of salt.

The intelligent question you should then ask yourself is this: If playing in that field is as daunting as they try to make you believe it is, why then are they still in it? Let me repeat, give no credence to their so-called 'expert advice'. Rather, go seek for a second, third, fourth and even fifth opinion before you even start to give what that first person said any iota of consideration. By the way, it is critical for you to be aware that even when you do seek alternative opinions, you must be certain that those you consult are not aspiring or lifelong members of the dreaded *Discouragement Committee*! I warn you; this kind of people are everywhere, so be very careful.

I heard this kind of talk a lot during the early days of my business, and I must confess that I was almost talked out of my dreams of building a successful business. I was almost convinced that I would be wasting my time to even make the effort.

Two things helped me survive this period. First, the five principles that I learnt from the school of hard knocks, and second, a disproportionate investment in my personal development. But for these two factors, I probably would not have had the courage to stay the course in my entrepreneurial quest to build a successful business.

Luckily for me, the discouragement I encountered had the opposite effect on me. Instead of causing me to throw in the towel, it rekindled within me a fierce desire to succeed. And armed with my thirst for knowledge, I soon discovered a commonality among all members of the *Discouragement Committee*. They all display the following five characteristics.

1. They fear competition because they are insecure.
2. They are ferocious about protecting their turf, so they ward off those they perceive as 'intruders'.
3. They have a scarcity mindset, and as a result, they are naturally wired to engage in self-preservation.

4. They are dissatisfied with how much of their potential they have utilized, and so naturally, they antagonize those attempting to maximize their potential.

5. They certainly do not have all the answers. They too are winging it and making it up as they go. They do not know half as much as they claim. Nobody really does.

As soon as I discovered these five underlying characteristics of people in the *Discouragement Committee,* their 'spell' lost its power, and I was better equipped to handle them whenever and wherever I encountered them.

As for the principles that helped me break through obstacles and enabled me to survive the dry start-up period of my business, they are universal principles. This means that they will without a doubt work for you and help you on your way to creating success.

The principles are:

1. **The Importance of Ability:** It is non-negotiable, you must become so good at what you do that most people will find it difficult to, legitimately and morally, deprive you of the opportunities you need to prove yourself. Please note the caveat, 'most people'. Some people will push the envelope, and no matter what you do and how good you are, will still do everything within their power to block you from those opportunities. The important thing to note here is this: in the end, those people do not matter in the grand scheme of things. There are more than enough opportunities out there, and as long as your skill is in demand, if you do not give up, you will eventually encounter thousands of people who will give you a chance. And when you do get the chance, make it count! Make yourself proud!

2. **The Importance of Work Ethics:** I have always known that I was not talented enough to avoid working hard, and this knowledge has served me extremely well. I strongly encourage you to adopt it. Till this day, I can outwork most people who I work with. In the pursuit of business success, there is absolutely no substitute for hard work. The sooner you embrace this fact, the faster you succeed.

3. **The Importance of Keeping Promises:** One of my favorite quotes of all time is, "if you do one thing well, people will assume you do everything well. If you do one thing poorly, people will assume you do everything poorly." This is especially true in business. Most times, you never get a second chance to make a great first impression. And first impressions matter a lot. Once you get a chance, make sure you go beyond the call of duty and ensure that promises made are promises kept.

4. **The Importance of Remaining a Life-long Student:** *The more you learn, the more you earn.* Although this is fast becoming a cliché, thankfully,

science has proven that knowledge indeed increases both wealth and well-being. A research done across 22 countries by the Organization for Economic Cooperation and Development (OECD), revealed that there is a remarkable correlation between skills and earnings, and an increase in skills *always* led to an increase in earnings. It is no longer news that globally, both in developing and developed economies, there is an ever-increasing demand for highly skilled labor and a shortage in supply of key talent. This shortage of talent means that there is more and more demand for people with exceptional skillsets, while the number of people who can fill those roles has remained constant. The natural consequence of this is that the wages of those who have highly demanded skillset increases. And this, my friend, is the reason why continuous learners will always remain high earners. So, you must become a lifelong learner if you hope to succeed against all odds. Whatever you do, don't ever, ever stop learning. Ever!

5. **The Importance of Serving Others:** "You will get all you want in life, if you help enough other people get what they want." This quote, attributed to Zig Ziglar, is so true. If you find yourself in a difficult place, if you are stuck and do not know the way out, find someone or a business whose need you can help meet. Go ahead and focus on helping them succeed rather than wallowing in your misery. This change of focus from self to others is what will liberate you. It is a spiritual principle, and it is also a business principle. When you focus on helping other people or businesses succeed, you unavoidably provide value, and the more value you provide, the more your worth increases. At the least, the following three things will play out in your favor:

Service opens your network. When you reach out to people or businesses that are not within your usual network to provide them with valuable support, it almost always marks the beginning of deep and meaningful relationships. Nothing contributes to the growth of a business than the network of its owner. The wider, larger, and more powerful your network is, the easier it will be for you to achieve success.

Word of genuine service spreads fast. Authentic acts of service always draws attention, especially in a world that is increasingly selfish. And who knows who may take notice of your generosity.

Acts of service reciprocate themselves. There is a foundational law of sowing and reaping programmed into the earth, and without anyone's help, it always plays out. Always! When you sow powerful service, it reaps for you powerful rewards.

These five principles served me well at the beginning of my entrepreneurial journey, and they still serve me well. Adopt and run with them, they will serve you as well as you run and build your business or career, especially in the face of discouragement and even outright attack on your dreams.

The truth is that you do not need any permission whatsoever from anyone to pursue your dreams whatever they might be. Stop thinking you need people's endorsements. Believe me when I say this, most external endorsements are grossly overrated. So, buckle up, stay the course, and do not allow yourself to get discouraged. Do not ever allow anyone steal your dreams. And whatever you do, DO NOT take permission from, or allow people to tell you what you can or cannot do.

Whatever you do, please do not be so naive as to believe that people will want you to succeed in an area where they desire to play but lack the courage to step into because of the fear of the unknown.

• **Key Takeaways**

- You do not need the validation of others to pursue your dreams.

- If pessimistic 'elders' in your field or area of interest (I call them members of the *Discouragement Committee*), have ever gone to great lengths to tell you how challenging and impossible it is to advance in that profession and how much of a mistake it would be to try, please take their advice with a pinch of salt. Seek for a second, third, fourth and even fifth opinion.

- Members of the Discouragement Committee have five things in common. They:

  i. Are insecure, therefore they fear competition.
  ii. Are ferocious about protecting their turf, so they ward off those they perceive as 'intruders'.
  iii. Have a scarcity mindset, and so they are naturally wired to engage in self-preservation.
  iv. Are dissatisfied with how much of their potential they have utilized, and so naturally, they antagonize those that attempt to maximize their potential.
  v. Do not know half as much as they claim. Nobody does.

- Do not be discouraged by these people. Instead, maximize the following five principles to help you break through any obstacle and enable you to survive the dry startup period of your business:

  i. Develop strong abilities and unquestionable competence in your field.
  ii. Demonstrate strong work ethics.
  iii. Keep your promises to yourself and others.
  iv. Be a life-long student
  v. Serve others

CHAPTER 26

THE ULTIMATE LIFE LESSON

"When it's time to die, let us not discover that we have never lived."
- Henry David Thoreau

Often, the hardest thing in the world for us to change is how we think and what we believe. While this is understandable, considering that our beliefs are tightly interwoven with our sense of identity, I have found that when beliefs are faulty, it becomes very dangerous to rigidly cling on to them. I am unreservedly certain about this because one of such faulty beliefs almost cost me a beautiful life.

It took a long time for me to realize that the way I thought about the past, the future and the present was unproductive. For most of my adult life, I lived mostly in the future and sometimes in the past; hardly ever did I spend quality time living in the present. And as is expected of all negative thinking habits, this caused me a great deal in my personal life and in my business, and to put it in the words of Henry David Thoreau, "I was one of the mass of men who lived a life of quiet desperation."

When it became glaring to me that something needed to change in the way I related with the past, present and future, the lifelong student in me embarked on a journey to unlearn and relearn how to live. During this journey, I reflected deeply on my experiences and those of others, and it was in the process of this life assessment and observation that I happened upon what I am now convinced is the most tragic way to live.

It became clear to me that the greatest injustice we can do to ourselves is to form the habit of 'postponing our lives', or 'waiting to live'. Without a doubt, the mindset of waiting to arrive at some utopian destination before we truly enjoy our life, instead of living in the present moment, is potentially one of the most devastating ways of thinking and belief that we can possess. This kind of thinking robs us of life because life is lived now, not later. *If you wait before you live, all that happens is that you will get older.* For some reason, in all our rationalizations, we have failed to truly see that when we remain fixated on tomorrow, we lose the present moment. When we keep fiddling and fretting about the future, we give up on the present and consequently, an entire lifetime!

This tragic habit of ours was best captured by the Roman Philosopher, Lucius Annaeus Seneca,_when he said: "They lose the day in expectation of the night, and the night in fear of the dawn." Even if we have the good fortune of a long and healthy life, how much fun can you possibly have when you are old and grey?

I once read a profound writeup titled, *The Station*, in which the author described human beings as being on a mythical train of life, rolling relentlessly down the tracks towards the future. As we travel on this train of life, we keep believing that just around the next bend, we are going to arrive at the Station, a beautiful little red station house that will signify the ultimate moment when all the pieces of our lives will fit together like completed jigsaw puzzles. When we arrive at the Station, there will be a big crowd cheering, flags waving, bands playing, and that is when all our goals will be achieved, and all our desires fulfilled. But there is only one big problem with the story: there is no Station! It is all a lie, pure unadulterated fantasy. The Station does not exist. The journey is what is important and if you fail to enjoy the ride in hopes that you will finally be able to have fun at the destination, you are making the biggest mistake of your life.

The truth is that you never quite arrive at 'The Destination'. There is always one more goal to reach, one more thing to do, one more accomplishment to see through and therefore, you must do everything you can to ensure you live in the moment. The best day to live your life to the fullest, to be unbelievably happy, to enjoy yourself and have some fun is today! If you keep waiting for your retirement to begin to do those things that make for a happiness-filled daily life, you may wistfully find that you have waited too long, and as one writer aptly said, "How late it is to begin to live when we must cease to live."

Time Waits For No One!

In Gary W. Keller and Jay Papasan's book, *The ONE Thing*, one of them tells a story that his wife told him about a friend of hers. "The friend's mother was a schoolteacher, and her father was a farmer. They had scrimped, saved, and done with less their entire lives in anticipation of retirement and travel. The woman fondly remembered the regular shopping trips she and her mother would take to the local fabric store where they would pick out some fabric and patterns. The mother explained that when she retired these would be her travel clothes. She never got to her retirement years. In her final year of teaching, she developed cancer and later died. The father never felt good about spending the money they'd saved, believing that it was 'their' money and now she wasn't there to share it with him. When he passed away and my wife's friend went to clean out her parents' home, she discovered a closet full of fabric and dress patterns. The father had never cleaned it out. He couldn't. It represented too much. It was as if its contents were so full of unfulfilled promises that they were too heavy to lift."

Time truly waits for no one.

One day I will ...

I used to be a 'One day I will' oriented person especially with respect to living the type of life I wanted to live. For instance, as a huge football fan, one of my dreams while growing up was to go watch the World Cup live every 4 years once I start working and making enough money to go. So far, I have had the means and resources to watch the last 4 World Cup games, but I have missed all four of them. I kept changing my plans because something always came up, there was always one new deal to chase and to close, one programme to attend, one pending problem to fix, etc., and the years trickled by. Then the pandemic struck, the lockdown was enforced, and gathering of crowds was banned. As I write this chapter, the pandemic is still on at a global scale and the prospects of ever having a large gathering of people again seem low, given the present circumstances. Every day the thought that my dream of watching the World Cup live might never be realized hits hard, and I keep asking myself, does this mean that I may never get to watch a World Cup Final live? It is a crushing feeling.

This is just one example out of several things I had planned to do when I finally arrived at my so-called 'destination', whatever that meant per time. I have learnt my lesson and I have promised myself, never again to postpone living till tomorrow. I will seize each moment and make the most of everyday. No matter what comes, I will seize every moment of my life.

Even though it has taken me this long to fully embrace the common saying that "in life, problems never cease", or like the Warri people of Nigeria, say powerfully in pidgin English, "*problem no dey finish*", going forward, I plan to live strictly by this powerful philosophy.

MD Scott Peck, in his bestselling book *The Road Less Travelled*, started the book with this profound statement, "Life is difficult." This is a fact and therefore, postponing the day you will enjoy your life is kryptonite to your superman tendencies.

Learning to live one happy, fulfilled, fun filled, productive and successful day at a time is the ultimate lesson that I believe all of us need to learn and live by. By all means, dream big, make big plans, have short-, medium- and long-term goals. Develop the 3, 5, 10-year visions for your life. But be sure to learn to live one successful day at a time.

Those who wish their lives away in anticipation of achieving some future goals do themselves a grave disservice. In the end, they will fully appreciate the wisdom of Lucius Annaeus Seneca's words when he said, "It is not that we have so little time but that we lose so much... The life we receive is not short, but we make it so; we are not ill provided but use what we have wastefully."

So, let me ask you: *How much of your life have you already lost waiting?*

Understand that life is not lost by dying, life is lost minute by minute, one unfulfilled day followed by another unfulfilled day.

I sincerely hope that you do not do yourself the disservice of waiting to live. Live now! For life is now. Life is not later. How truly tragic it is that too often, "a very old man has no other proof of his long life than his age" – Seneca the Younger.

Key Takeaways

- The greatest injustice we can do to ourselves is to form the habit of 'postponing our lives', or 'waiting to live'. Without a doubt, the mindset of waiting to arrive at some utopian destination before we truly enjoy our lives, in the present moment, is the most potentially devastating thinking and belief we can possess. This kind of thinking robs us of life because life is now, not later.

- The truth is that you never quite arrive at 'The Destination'. There is always one more goal to reach, one more thing to do, one more accomplishment to see through and that is why you must do all you can to ensure you live in the moment. The best day to live your life to the fullest, to be unbelievably happy, to enjoy yourself and have some fun is today!

- Learning to live one happy, fulfilled, fun filled, productive and successful day at a time is the ultimate lesson that I believe all human beings need to live by. Dream big, make big plans, have short-, medium- and long-term goals. Develop visions for the next 3, 5 or 10 years. But learn to live one successful day at a time.

- Life is not lost by dying, life is lost minute by minute, one unfulfilled day by another unfulfilled day. Live now! How truly tragic it is that too "often, a very old man has no other proof of his long life than his age."

- How much of your life have you already lost waiting?

CONCLUSION

YOU CAN BEAT THE ODDS IN LIFE AND BUSINESS AND YOU SHOULD

"Chiefly, the mold of a man's fortune is in his own hands."

- Francis Bacon

The business of people is a very revealing business. When I relate with people in my capacity as a coach, mentor, trainer, and consultant, I meet a version of humanity that is unmasked, open and real. I have met with people who were at their highest points, and people who were at their lowest ebbs. I have listened to people with deep regrets, and I have shared in the excitement of people with deep satisfaction. Through it all, I have observed closely, and I have reflected. I have seen repeated patterns in those who are deeply satisfied with the outcomes of their lives and identified similarities in the choices of those who have despaired over the decisions that they made and did not make. If I were to sum up the insight that I have gained from what has been a 15-year personal study, it will be this: *An ownership mentality gives birth to an empowered life and an entitlement mentality aborts every chance of a glorious life.*

Simply put, we are all products of our mentalities.

Each time that I listened to those with regrets, these words of Napoleon Hill always echoed in my mind, "Men and women who come to the closing chapter of life disappointed because they did not attain the goal which they had set their hearts upon achieving, they teach you what not to do."

And what *not* to do is to run your entire life with the mentality that the world owes you something for nothing, and that comfort is to be prioritized above growth. This mentality cripples destinies, and I mean this literally.

The *Entitlement Mentality* which says, "I can't kill myself, what will be will be; what is my own will come to me," drives those that cleave to it to live passive and entitled lives, lives that end up full of dissatisfaction and regrets.

The *Comfort Zone Mentality* that says, "This is too hard, something must be wrong with it. There must be an easier way out", motivates those that hold to it to keep putting their dreams on hold while they search for a hack, and the easiest way out. Sadly, there are no easy roads to success and easy streets will take you where you do not want to go.

I wrote this book to extoll the virtues of the *Ownership Mentality*, the mentality that says, "I own this! I've got this! No extraordinary result ever came from mediocre effort." This mentality motivates those that live by it to embrace the discipline that brings progress, the hard work, toil, repeated practice, and continuous and unending learning and self-improvement that births success.

When we read the stories of people who not only survived devastating situations but went on to thrive and lead very successful lives, we stand in awe of such people. When we read rag-to-riches stories, of impossible situations that became possible, we revel in such stories. But behind every single one of such success stories is a journey filled with minutes, hours, days, weeks, months, and years of grueling ownership thinking and acting. I have repeatedly found that many times when life deals a person with an extreme blow, only a commensurate response of extreme ownership thinking and acting brings happy endings. Nothing, absolutely nothing can happen if we do not take responsibility for our lives. In the same way, absolutely anything is possible when we accept responsibility for everything in our lives. In the moment when we take ownership for our outcomes, we gain the power to change anything and everything, as far as is humanly possible. I am utterly convinced that ownership thinking and acting answers many problems under the sun.

As an employee, if you care for your organization as much as the owner of the organization does, if you work harder than the owner, sacrifice more than the owner, keep learning and improving yourself more than the owner, build connections, etc., you will inevitably become an owner yourself. The eternal laws of the Universe are programmed to produce that result for you.

As a business owner, if you make your products or services more valuable than your competitors, if you do the work and become a master in a world filled with half-baked apprentices, if you face your reality with courage and build your strategy to respond to that reality, if you stay inspired and perfect the art of keeping things simple, if you leverage the forces of mentorship, goal setting, productive habits, and powerful connections, you will always top your industry.

If you take ownership of the smallest details of your personal life, if you pay the full price that is required to achieve success in your work, relationships, and health, if you initiate the force of creative thinking in your life by asking and answering powerful and bold questions, questions that demand that you hold yourself to the highest standards, your entire life will begin to change as you decide that you will no longer accept mediocrity for yourself. These questions include:

- *Is this all that there is to me?*
- *Is this truly all that I am capable of?*
- *Is this all I can really do?*
- *Is this what I want to be for the rest of my life?*
- *Is this acceptable to me?*

I am yet to meet one successful person who got successful by sitting all day long, just wishing and hoping to accomplish great things. Every single person I have met with substantial results, spectacular achievements and laudable accomplishments started off by taking ownership for creating that success. They consistently and persistently took purposeful, meaningful, and well-thought-out steps.

Powerful things begin to happen when you take responsibility for the outcomes of your life. When you activate the force of ownership thinking and acting, first your will and intellect unify, then your values, thoughts, feelings, and actions align. When all these critical components line up, it will birth in you a fierce hunger, an unquenchable desire to succeed. When you get to this point, half the battle is won because few things can withstand the giant capacity that laser focus and fierce determination bring into every situation, no matter how dire it may be. All achievements of mankind are a testament to this.

The only thing that can really stop you is fear. And remember what I said in the lesson on making failure an ally, you must never fear failure. Instead, fear living your life in such a way that makes regret inevitable.

"It might have been," are the saddest words that anyone can utter when their days on earth are complete.

In his book *Dead Toad Scrolls*, Kilroy J. Oldster perceptively noted that regrets in life comes in four tones.

First, we regret the life that we lived and the decisions we made.

Second, we regret the life we did not live, the opportunities missed, the adventures postponed indefinitely.

Third, we regret that parts of our life are over; we hang onto nostalgic feelings for the past, when everything was new.

Fourth, we experience bitterness because the world did not prove to be what we hoped or expected it to be.

What a blessing it would be to avoid all four regrets!

If you operate your life from the *Ownership Zone*, if you walk the road less travelled, if you diligently follow the precepts of *Ownership Thinking and Acting* as conveyed in the lessons in this book, you will not only avoid all four regrets, but you will also get results that few people get. You will beat the odds in life and in business.

Therefore, take ownership of your life. Become the commander-in-chief of all the divisions in your life. Charge into your future with fury, attack every waking moment with a ferocity that no opposition can withstand. Care more than others think is wise, be willing to work longer, harder, and smarter. Become a learning machine and take control of your destiny. Have a clear vision that is backed by definite plans. Not only is it possible to do this, when you do it, it will birth in and for you a power, a freedom, a joy, a fullness of life, and a satisfaction that you never thought possible.

Begin today to take those steps that are necessary to securing your future, steps that will ensure that rather than *owing* your future, you OWN it!

Nothing truly stands in your way.

BEAT THE ODDS AND SUCCEED

To take ownership of your career and business

Visit

OwnersInstitute.com

ABOUT OWNERS' INSTITUTE

At Owners' Institute, we are on a mission to grow the next generation of Owners and Ownership-driven enterprises in Africa. We exist to help individuals and businesses in Africa realize their full potential.

Owners' Institute is a practical business school (minus the academic theories) for **established entrepreneurs** who want to grow & scale their businesses, **emerging entrepreneurs** who want to make the transition from employee to entrepreneurs, **enterprising experts** who want to monetize their expertise by starting their own side hustle, and businesses that seek to become ownership-oriented organizations.

Too many businesses are failing at an astronomical rate across Africa, and those left standing are either struggling or performing mediocrely at best. Though we hate that this happens, we understand why it happens. The fact is that growing a business is hard. In Africa, it is even more grueling. It is akin to running a marathon. And like marathon champion, Juma Ikangaa once said:

"The will to win means nothing without the will to prepare."

This is what we are about at the Owners' Institute. We exist to help you prepare in such a way that winning in today's cutthroat business world becomes inevitable.

As a community-based platform, we provide practical training, tools, coaching and support for individuals and businesses within our vibrant communities to enable them beat the odds and succeed where others are struggling.

Visit **www.ownersinstitute.com** to get started

Tweet at us: **@owners_Inst**

Send a DM: **OwnersInstitute_**

Connect on LinkedIn: **Owners Institute**

Follow on Facebook: **Owners Institute**

Send a mail: **oteam@ownersinstitute.com**

We care about you.

We want you to succeed.

ABOUT THE AUTHOR

Bolaji Olagunju is a serial entrepreneur, angel investor, author, trainer, coach, mentor, and consultant to some of the most important and interesting businesses in Africa.

He is the Founder and Executive Chairman of Workforce Group (www. workforcegroup.com)_ - one of the leading Business & HR Consulting firms in Africa, made up of multiple subsidiaries offering business advisory, learning & development, outsourcing, recruitment & assessment, and market entry & operations support. Workforce Group is present in 7 African countries, it has a staff strength of over 8000 people, and it is headquartered at the The Zone (www.thezone.ng), a world-class purpose-built facility hired out to businesses for serviced private offices, meetings, trainings, hybrid conferences, retreats, strategy sessions, team building and corporate events.

Bolaji is also the Founder of Ownersinstitute.com, a pragmatic membership-based learning and growth community for established entrepreneurs, emerging entrepreneurs, subject matter experts who want to monetize their expertise and ownership-oriented organizations.

He is a co-founder in several technology start-ups including: Learnry (a Learning Management System), Outwork (a task management solution), AllDay HR (a Human Resource Software for large corporations and SMEs) mAudition (an innovative video application designed purely for entertainment.)

Bolaji is an alumnus of Lagos Business School, and he has attended several programs in leading universities all over the world, including Berkeley Haas School of Business, Colombia Business School, Michigan Ross Business School, Kellogg Business School, and UNC Kenan-Flagler Business School.

He is the author of two best-selling books— Hiring Right: A Matter of Life and Death for Businesses, Business Owners and Executives (www.hiringrightbook.

com) and You Must Become a Trainer: How to leverage your expertise, experience and education in any field to do what you love, impact lives, create wealth and own your future. Both books have been widely acclaimed as practical manuals for business executives in Africa.

Mr. Olagunju is passionate about learning, teaching, job creation, making people employable and mentoring entrepreneurs. In just a few short years, he transformed Workforce Management Centre into Workforce Group, made up of more than 6 subsidiaries and grew the business to multiple-seven figures in revenue. Together with his team of 20+ people spread all over the world, he now leads a mission to support a very special global community of 10,000+ loyal and inspired entrepreneurs.